WITHDRAWN

D0478164

Paper Made!

101 Exceptional Projects to Make
Out of Everyday Paper

KAYTE TERRY

WORKMAN PUBLISHING · NEW YORK

DEDICATION

This book is dedicated to Adam and Potato.

Copyright © 2012 by Kayte Terry
Illustration copyright © by Sophie Nicolay

All rights reserved. No portion of this book may
be reproduced—mechanically, electronically, or
by any other means, including photocopying—
without written permission of the publisher.
Published simultaneously in Canada by Thomas
Allen & Son Limited.

Library of Congress Cataloging-in-Publication
Data is available.

ISBN 978-0-7611-5997-1

Cover design by Raquel Jaramillo
Design by Lidija Tomas

Workman books are available at special
discounts when purchased in bulk for
premiums and sales promotions as well as
for fund-raising or educational use. Special
editions or book excerpts also can be created
to specification. For details, contact the Special
Sales Director at the address below, or send
an e-mail to specialmarkets@workman.com.

Workman Publishing Company, Inc.
225 Varick Street
New York, NY 10014-4381
www.workman.com

Printed in the United States of America
First printing April 2012

10 9 8 7 6 5 4 3 2 1

PHOTO CREDITS

Front Cover
From top left to right: Songbird Votive, Deborah Ory; Prizewinning
Bowl and First-Prize Paper Ribbons, Melissa Lucier; Cardboard, Robyn
Mackenzie/shutterstock; Scissors, Tribalium/shutterstock; bottom left
to right: portrait, Adam Louie; frame, Melissa Lucier, Deborah Ory, Elena
Schweitzer/shutterstock

Back Cover
From left to right: Timurock/fotolia, Tribalium/shutterstock, Melissa Lucier

Author portrait by Deborah Ory

Interior
Prop stylist: Sara Abalan

Photography by Deborah Ory
p.iv, p.viii, pp.xi–xii, p.xvi, p.4, p.11, p.12 main image, p.14 bottom, p.17 top,
p.18, pp.21–22, pp.26–32, pp.36–38, p.41 top, p.44, pp.49–56, pp.65–67,
pp.70–78, p.85, p.86, pp.88–93, pp.100–103, p.106, p.114, p.117, p.120,
p.122, pp.127–129, p.135 right, p.136, p.139, p.152, p.155, p.158, p.160, p.163,
pp.169–175, pp.180–184, p.187, p.190, pp.196–200, pp.203–208, p.212,
p.224, pp.226–239

Additional photography
Adam Louie: p.69; Melissa Lucier: p.i, pp.v–vii, p.ix–x, pp.xiii–xiv, p.14 top,
p.16 bowl, pp.24–25, pp.33–35, p.40, p.41 bottom, p.42, pp.46–47, p.58, p.59
top, pp.60–64, pp.68–69 (frame), pp.81–83, p.84 bottom, p.87, pp.94–95,
p.96 right, pp.97–99, pp.104–105, pp.107–113, p.115, p.119, p.121, pp.124–125,
pp.130–135 left, p.138, pp.140–145, pp.147–149, p.150 top, p.151, p.157, p.162,
pp.164–167, pp.176–179, pp.186, pp.188–189, pp.192–194, p.195, p.202, p.211,
pp.214–223, p.225; Kayte Terry: p.12 inset, p.146; fotolia: Aaron Amat p.159, AJ
p.96 left, Nick Barounis p.2 left, Brebca p.42 baby, Diego Cervo p.59 bottom
left, Norman Chan p.153, clearviewstock p.59 bottom right, Bert Folsom p.2
middle, ksena32@ukrpost.ua p.3 top, Landysh p.xv, Olivier Le Moal p.139
ribbon, Lusia p.3 bottom, Sujit Mahapatra p.150, Alexander Maximov p.6
middle, Mirabella p.84 top, Picsfive p.16 cards, Bruce Shippe p.17 bottom,
slavapolo p.19, syolacan, thatchai p.2 right, Tjommy p.6 right, Serghei Velusceac
p.6 left; istock: p.195 curtains

Acknowledgments

I am so thankful to everyone who was involved in the making of this book.

To my awesomely talented and patient editor, Megan Nicolay, who helped me get this project off the ground; my agent, Stacey Glick, for always being by my side; and the super-fantastic team that made the photo shoot both stunning and fun: Anne Kerman, the photo director; Melissa Lucier, her assistant and the studio photographer; Deborah Ory, the photographer; Sara Albalan, the photo stylist; and Parcel and Gypsy Farmhouse, for their props.

To Janet Vicario, for her art directing prowess; Lidija Tomas, for the beautiful design; Sophie Nicolay, for making the illustrations both beautiful and easy to follow (not a small task!); and James Williamson, for his work on the templates.

To my friends near and far, for ideas, support, late-night phone calls, crafty retreats, and just being awesome.

To my awesome and growing family and family-in-law, and especially to my mother, for always cheering me on and being in my corner—even when I have no time to visit because I'm always working (sorry Mom!)! A big thanks to my grandmothers, whom I lost while working on this book, for their style, wit, and inspiration. I miss you terribly!

To Potato, my rabbit and muse, for his constant crafty assistance and paper scrap eating/recycling.

And most of all to Adam, who has been my partner in life and craft through three books now and still doesn't complain when the house gets turned upside down with craft projects.

Contents

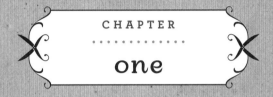

CHAPTER
one

All the basic tools and techniques you need for working with paper.

CHAPTER
two

A guide to thinking outside of the (cardboard) box—where to get materials,

clever tool hacks, and how to save and store your paper scraps.

CHAPTER
three

NEW WORLD
DICTIONARY
of the American Language
Students Edition

CHAPTER
four

CHAPTER

five

Paper for Wrapping and Writing

CHAPTER
· · · · · · · · · · ·
six

Introduction

For many of us, making things with paper is our first venture into the world of arts and crafts. As a child, I remember creating masks and hats from paper plates, snipping paper into snowflakes, and looping long chains of garlands from colorful construction paper. It seemed like magic, the number of things that could be made from a new pad of paper.

I grew up in a family of artists who saw creative potential in everything: Discarded oatmeal cans and cereal boxes could be musical instruments, and stacks of old cardboard boxes doubled as elaborate forts. Years later, I'm still captivated by the possibilities of paper. As a visual merchandiser and display artist, I've constructed chandeliers from folded book pages, sewn dresses made of wallpaper and paint chips, and even covered a whole room in papier-mâché!

So it seems a great understatement to simply say that paper is an incredibly versatile raw material: It can be folded, rolled, sculpted, shredded, cut, and sewn. With paper, you can make stationery, jewelry, home decor, and even furniture—and you don't need a whole slew of fancy, expensive tools! In fact, many of the paper projects in this book require only glue and a good cutting tool—and paper is often free (or nearly so) for the taking. Look to your recycling bin for piles of old magazines, cardboard, newspapers, and phone books. Thrift stores and flea markets are great places to find old maps, wallpaper scraps, letters, and other vintage ephemera. Upcycling old bits and pieces of paper is not only a creative way to craft for less, it's also the responsible thing to do for our environment. By giving these scraps new purpose, you are extending the usefulness of the materials and keeping them out of the trash. It's really a win-win situation!

At the start of this tradition of turning old into new was the first paper, created in China circa A.D. 105, which was made from upcycled bits of old mulberries, rags, and hemp. This early paper was intended as a surface for writing and recording information, but eventually everyone caught on to the variety of uses for paper. Chinese paper dating from the second and third centuries has been found in such forms as packing materials, tea bags, money, and even very early toilet paper!

Because paper is a readily available and relatively inexpensive material to work with, it has been incorporated into a number of folk art traditions around the globe. Talk about well-traveled: From Polish *pajaki* (see page 228) to Japanese origami (see pages 114, 150, and 238) to German *Scherenschnitte* (page 62), people the world over can't get enough of paper crafting.

In these pages, you'll find all the techniques you need to know to start crafting with paper—plus how to make 101 paper projects for hosting stylish parties, decorating a hip home, and making fashion-forward accessories. There are simple, fun projects that take an hour or two, more complicated projects that will take you a couple of days, and everything in between. And perhaps best of all, every single one of these projects can be made with recycled, repurposed, or scrap paper. So let's get started and see all the things that paper can do.

Happy crafting!

CHAPTER

one

THE BASICS: IT'S ALL IN THE TECHNIQUE

Grab a sheet of paper and hold it in your hands. Think of all the things you can do with it: Crumple it, fold it, rip it, paint it, weave it, stitch it. Tear paper into strips to make papier-mâché, or cut it into intricate designs. Each sheet of paper contains endless possibilities.

In this chapter, you'll learn some of the myriad techniques for working with paper and be introduced to the basic tools required for these techniques. From the traditional folding, cutting, and pasting to the more unexpected paper stitching and jewelry constructing, the following pages detail some of the types of paper craft you'll be learning about.

Cut and Paste

Decoupage comes from the French word *découper,* meaning "to cut." In the craft of decoupage, shapes and images are cut out of paper and applied to another surface with glue. When decoupage is done well, the images look painstakingly painted rather than simply glued. Decoupage was enormously popular during Victorian times, and images were produced specifically to cut out for decoupaging. Although scrolls, flowers, and angels were the popular images then, decoupage can include any designs and patterns you choose. You can cut geometric shapes out of tissue paper, motifs from wallpaper scraps, or use your own illustrations.

Cutting, in decoupage, can be done with a craft knife and cutting mat (see the following section, "Cut It Out") or sharp scissors. I prefer using the craft knife when working with images because I can cut more quickly and have more control when moving around detailed edges, but a small pair of scissors can easily do the trick too.

White glue, also known as *PVA glue,* is a wonderful, nontoxic, acid-free glue that's best used as an adhesive and not as a sealant.

Mod Podge and other *decoupage mediums,* also nontoxic, act as both glues and sealants, which make them the better options for projects where you need both. Don't you just love a good multitasking craft supply?

If you decide to decoupage a piece of furniture or another item that will get a lot of wear and tear, I recommend also sealing with *polyurethane* or an *acrylic spray.* Depending on the look you want, you can choose from matte, semigloss, or gloss. All are easy to find at a craft or hardware store. Keep in mind, however, that although acrylic spray is the best choice in order to get professional results, it's not the most environmentally friendly.

A *brayer* looks like a miniature rolling pin and is essential for smoothing decoupage images and removing paper wrinkles and excess glue. Find one in the printmaking section at most craft and art supply stores.

A *foam paintbrush* is inexpensive and won't leave brushstrokes when you apply the decoupage medium. Buy the brushes by the bagful and store them in your craft area.

Cut It Out

Paper cutting, the art of cutting designs out of paper, has evolved in various ways around the world, with countries as different as Poland and China developing their own particular styles.

There are many, many types of paper that are excellent for cutting, including magazines, wallpaper, and copy paper. However, I do recommend avoiding paper that is either too thin (tissue paper will tear easily) or too thick (such as card stock), as well as handmade paper that has a distinct texture (while textured paper is beautiful, it's difficult to cut with precision). Why make your life more difficult?

Paper cuts are often extremely intricate, but only a few tools are needed for this craft. Most paper cuts are made with a very sharp *craft knife* (or *X-ACTO knife*) and a *self-healing cutting mat* in order to achieve precise results. I prefer a knife to scissors for certain projects that require that precision, plus I can cut more quickly. The self-healing cutting mat protects your work surface and prevents your knife blade from getting dull. If you don't have a cutting mat, a big piece of corrugated cardboard works in a pinch.

A few styles of paper cutting, such as making snowflakes or paper chains, are easier with a small pair of *all-purpose scissors.* The key here is having a sharp pair, since you may be cutting through multiple sheets of paper at a time.

In addition to traditional scissors, there is now a wide variety of *decorative-edge scissors* and *paper punches* to mimic the delicate look of paper cutting. You don't *need* any of these tools, but they can make a lot of projects (like O Happy Day Banner, page 186, and *Pająki* Chandelier, page 228) easier and faster.

Want to cut through several pieces of paper at once? *Binder clips* do a great job of holding papers in place while cutting, much better than your fingers ever will.

In Stitches

I love to sew on paper. It adds an unexpected texture and beautiful detail to craft projects. You can sew on pretty much any paper, but avoid anything that's too thin (because it may tear) or too thick (it's just too hard to get it through the machine!).

It's relatively easy to use a *sewing machine* to stitch or embroider on paper—just exchange the standard fabric needle for a *leather needle.* (But remember to change the needle again before you switch back to sewing fabric!)

To hand embroider on paper, mark your design with a pencil on the right side of your work, then poke holes along the pencil lines with a *sewing needle* before you start to stitch. That way, when you are stitching your paper, you are not blindly poking into the wrong side of the paper. Since paper isn't as forgiving as fabric (any needle holes are permanent!), this gives you a much neater end product. Most of the time, your pencil lines won't be visible after you have stitched over them, but you can lightly erase any stray marks at the end. *Embroidery floss* works best for paper stitching because it's thicker than thread and won't easily pull through the holes.

To embellish paper with sewn sequins, beads, or buttons, mark your stitch holes the same way you would with hand embroidery: Thread the needle, knot the thread end, and bring the needle up  through a stitch hole in the paper. Then bring the needle through a hole in the embellishment, switch the direction of the needle, and bring it back down through the embellishment via a second hole. Finally, bring the needle through the original stitch hole to secure the embellishment to the paper. Secure the threads with a small knot and a dab of glue on the back of the paper.

Speaking of knots, there are tons of different kinds of knots, but for the thread work in this book you really only need to know how to do one: the overhand knot. Here's how:

1. Hold one end of the string or thread in your left hand. With your right hand, make a loop (or an eye) at the end of the string. The string will form an X at the bottom of the loop where it crosses itself.

2. Hold the X with your left hand and use your right hand to poke the end of the string through the eye, then pull taut.

3. Pull the end taut to tighten and complete the knot.

If a project calls for a double overhand knot, it just means that you repeat those steps to make a second knot over the first. I'll indicate which knot is preferable for each project.

Back to the Fold

By folding and creasing, you can create something sculptural from a flat sheet of paper. While paper folding is a folk art in many cultures (and is believed to have originated in China with the invention of paper),

Up to Fold Tricks

Master origami maker Dinh Giang (http://giangdinh.com) has a way with paper that few others can claim. In addition to the folds of traditional origami, Giang uses the wet-folding technique, dampening the paper as he sculpts to add curved sculptural elements to his work. Intricately folded faces, figures, and animals come to life in his hands.

the Japanese art of origami is the best-known of these traditions. In origami, you can make almost anything, from the ubiquitous paper crane to decorative frogs, dinosaurs, and umbrellas, plus functional items such as boxes and bins.

Folded paper projects require few tools, making them extremely portable (an excellent craft to pack and take on a trip!). The most important tools for accurate paper folding are a *ruler* and a *bone folder*. Rulers are essential for marking straight folds. A bone folder is a flat, blunt tool that helps you make crisp, clean creases in paper. If you don't have a bone folder, substitute the handle of a butter knife, the back of a pair of scissors, or a ruler.

Most paper is relatively flexible and easy to fold, but when you're working with heavyweight paper like cardboard, you'll need to *score* it first to properly manipulate it. When you score paper, you essentially cut halfway through it. Using a sharp craft knife on a self-healing cutting mat, cut gently and evenly into the paper, taking care never to cut all the way through. After you score it, you can easily bend the paper and create all sorts of wonderful three-dimensional projects!

Some papers have a distinct grain (referring to the direction of the paper particles) and need to be folded with, or parallel to, the grain in order to achieve a neat fold. One way to determine the grain is to tear a small sample of the paper. If you tear *with*

the grain, the paper will rip easily and in a moderately straight line. If you tear *against* the grain, the paper will resist and the tears will be jagged and uneven. If your paper has a distinct grain, orient it so you can fold it in a direction that is parallel to the grain—your creases will be neat as a pin.

Sometimes when folding and cutting paper, I will ask you to *miter* your corners. What the heck is mitering? It's a lot simpler than it sounds. In the world of paper cutting, mitering simply means to cut a corner at a 45-degree angle. This is a handy little trick to use when covering an object with paper (see the Two Types of Stripes Switch Plates, page 24, for instance) because it eliminates some of the extra bulk that results when you wrap the paper around an object. A mitered corner makes for a cleaner finish.

In basic origami folding, there are two terms to become familiar with. A *mountain fold* and a *valley fold* can be made at any angle on a sheet of paper (horizontally, vertically, or on any diagonal in between) and are inverses of each other. A mountain fold is traditionally represented by a dashed line *and* looks like this:

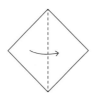

mountain fold

A valley fold is represented by a dashed and dotted line and looks like this:

valley fold

Papier-Mâché

"Papier-mâché" is a French term meaning "chewed-up paper" (sounds better in French, huh?) that refers to both the material and technique. Traditionally, papier-mâché is made by soaking paper in room-temperature water until it becomes a pulpy clay. I prefer to make papier-mâché the way we did back in grade school, with *torn strips of newspaper* and *glue and water* or a *flour and water mixture*.

To make a papier-mâché form, you can either work over an existing item or create your own structure with chicken wire. If you are working over an existing item such as a bowl, make sure to cover the bowl in plastic first. This will protect the bowl and will also make it easy to remove the papier-mâché form when you're done. Traditionally, *balloons* also make great rounded forms for  papier-mâché. I use punching ball balloons for some projects because they are perfectly round.

Beads and Baubles: A Jewelry-Making 101

The jewelry-making projects in this book feature very easy techniques even if you are a complete novice, but you are going to have to know about a few special tools and supplies beyond those traditionally associated with paper crafting.

There are two kinds of pliers called for in this book: *flat-nose* and *round-nose pliers*. If you aren't making a career out of jewelry, it is pretty easy to find an inexpensive jewelry-making set of pliers at a craft store. They are fine for any of the projects you will find here.

Flat-nose pliers are used for opening up jump rings, and round-nose pliers are best for things like making loops and bending wire.

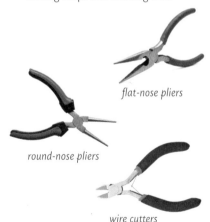

flat-nose pliers

round-nose pliers

wire cutters

Wire cutters are used to, you guessed it, cut wire. Again, no need to break the bank here. A small, inexpensive wire cutter will do the trick.

In jewelry, *jump rings* are metal rings that connect one piece to another, like a clasp to a chain or a *head pin* to an *earring wire*. They come in many metal finishes and sizes and are very easy to open and close with small flat-nose pliers. There is a right and wrong way to open them, though.

Gently twist one end down just enough to open the jump ring.

Do not pull one end away from the other. It will weaken the ring and be harder to restore the shape.

A head pin, frequently used when constructing jewelry, is basically a metal stick with a pin head or loop on the end of it to keep beads from slipping off. The wire end can be bent into a loop with needle-nose pliers to attach an earring wire or a jump ring. You can also easily use wire cutters to trim head pins into different sizes with wire cutters.

Earring wires are the part of the earring (that hooked piece of wire) that you stick into your ear. They're the functional part of an earring—and the defining component!

Jewelry adhesive is a superstrong permanent glue used in some types of jewelry making and embellishing. I recommend the brand E6000 because, well, it *works,* but I must warn you: This glue is pretty toxic. Use it sparingly and in a very well-ventilated area.

❖

Pattern Perfect

Since this book is all about reusing and recycling, the templates and patterns you'll need are all available online. Less paper to waste—more paper to craft with! Simply choose the pattern you'll need and print it out according to the instructions on the page. No need to worry about lost pattern pieces: You can always access them at workman.com/papermade.

two

MATERIALS:
BE RESOURCEFUL,
B-E RESOURCEFUL!

If I were a cheerleader, this would definitely be my cheer. Resourcefulness, to me, is next to godliness, an amazing (though often underrated) quality to possess.

You'd be surprised to find the number of materials and tools you already have within reach in your home and community! In fact, if you got really creative, you could probably stock your entire paper craft workshop without stepping foot in a store.

A lot of the projects in this book emphasize recycling and reusing, and in that spirit, many of your supplies can be found for free (or at least very cheaply) if you know where to look. Here's where I start.

The Recycling Bin

This is always my first stop for supplies. Magazines, greeting cards, cereal boxes and other food packaging, gift boxes, other cardboard containers, copy paper—all of these can have a second life in paper craft.

Freecycle or Craigslist

Do you need a large quantity of paper for a project? Maybe you're trying to make the world's longest gum wrapper chain and you don't like to chew gum. Put a request out there on either Freecycle.com or Craigslist.org and see what happens. Somewhere there's an obsessive gum chewer who would love to give you her wrappers.

Clear Your Mind— and Your Workspace

Okay, so you want to get started. First, let's make sure that you have a clean spot to get your craft on. Clear a surface on a table or on the floor and make sure to protect your work surface with newspaper or a cutting mat—this is supposed to be fun, not destructive! Most of the glues you will use in these projects are nontoxic. If you are working with spray adhesive or jewelry adhesive, make sure you open a window.

Friends and Family

If you need something and you don't have it, simply ask around! I don't get the Yellow Pages anymore, so when I needed one for a project, I sent an e-mail to some coworkers and, what do you know, one was sitting on my desk the next morning. One of my aunts is currently collecting toilet paper rolls so I can make another Secret Stash Beaded Curtain (page 54).

Okay, so you tried and tried to score some free supplies and you're still coming up short. Here's where I head next for supplies that are cheap and easy to repurpose.

Thrift Stores and Garage Sales

Not everything in life is free. Vintage paper ephemera, such as wallpaper scraps, old letters, books, and stamps, might be hard to get for free, but they are easy to find secondhand (by browsing the local yard, stoop, or garage sale) if you're willing to spend an hour or two rummaging through bins of old record sleeves, photos, and the like. And the goodies you find usually don't cost a lot.

eBay and Etsy

Secondhand paper items are very easy to score online. Sites such as eBay.com and Etsy.com allow you to travel to and shop at virtual yard sales across the country and world from the comfort of your craft room.

Still can't find what you need for free or on the cheap? The last stop on the resourceful train is buying new, but there are still some thrifty and eco-friendly options to consider.

Share with a Friend

Take up bookmaking or paper cutting with a friend and share your supplies. You can buy in bulk and there is far less waste.

Join a Skillshare Group or a Craft Night

Craft groups often have a shared materials pool that is available when the group meets. You shouldn't have to purchase new materials when you need them for just one project!

Let's say you really want to make the Paperback Riser (page 234) in Chapter 6, but you don't have a self-healing cutting mat (maybe you didn't even know what one was before you turned to page 2!). Never fear! Here are some simple materials that you probably have lying around the house that can be substituted in order to get the job done in a pinch.

• A piece of corrugated cardboard can take the place of a self-healing cutting mat. It doesn't heal like a cutting mat but that's okay—it's recyclable!

- Need to trace a perfect circle? Just look around and you'll see that you're surrounded by circles. I use spools of thread, cans, jar lids, and mixing bowls as templates.

- What in the world is a bone folder (see page 5)? I love my bone folder, but if you don't have one, the blunt end of a butter knife or the edge of a ruler subs in nicely.

- Binder and bulldog clips work as C-clamps. I use them to hold stacks of paper together for bookbinding or to hold pieces of paper in place while glue is drying.

- Painter's tape is also an excellent temporary adhesive because it peels easily without damaging paper. I use it to hold strips of paper in place while I'm weaving them (see One-Way Ticket Place Mat, page 32).

Save Your Scraps!

You will notice throughout this book that some of the same papers end up in multiple projects but are used in very different ways. That's because this book is all about saving and reusing all your paper scraps, and I want to lead by example. I keep every piece of paper that I find interesting, from cool packaging to little pieces of wallpaper, paint chips, postage stamps, even the inside of security envelopes (I'm not kidding—check out the patterns hiding inside—amazing!) and store them away for future use.

I organize my little scraps into larger envelopes by color and then the bigger pieces get filed by type (wallpaper, lined paper, card stock—you get the picture). Really large pieces of paper are best stored in a roll and—bonus!—they take up less space that way.

And did you know that you can compost paper scraps? Any paper that has been printed with soy-based inks can be composted. And that's a lot: Newspaper, paper towels, brown paper bags, envelopes, and cereal boxes, to name a few, can be tossed into the bin and turned into mulch.

SUPPLIERS

Although this book encourages working with used or found materials as much as possible, you will probably have to purchase a few new things (craft knife blades and glue come to mind). The following are some of my favorite suppliers (some are online and some have stores that you can visit in person, too).

A.C. Moore
(acmoore.com)
For all your general crafting needs, you can shop online or in-store at this small arts and crafts chain. Among other basic tools and materials, you can pick up thread and needles in their sewing section to arm yourself for the minimal amount of stitching in this book.

D. Blümchen & Company
(blumchen.com)
This is one of my favorite sources for vintage and vintage-inspired craft supplies: crepe paper, art paper, gold foil and seals, scrap pictures for decoupage, and lots more.

Dick Blick
(dickblick.com)
One-stop shopping for all your basic paper crafting supplies: craft knives, self-heating mats, rulers, papers galore, and many kinds of adhesives. The staff is often populated with art students who are knowledgeable about and familiar with the products.

Fire Mountain Gems and Beads
(firemountaingems.com)
This is my favorite jewelry findings supplier. Any jewelry notion from the materials lists in Paper's in Fashion (Chapter 4 of this book) can be found at Fire Mountain Gems.

Klockit
(klockit.com)
Everything you need to make your own clocks!

Nashville Wraps
(nashvillewraps.com)
Go here for tissue paper (and other gift wrapping needs) in dozens of gorgeous colors. Recommended by

the queen of crafts herself, Ms. Martha Stewart.

The Lamp Shop
(lampshop.com)

Everything you need to make your own lamps!

Michaels
(michaels.com)

Browse online for basic supplies, then find the nearest location of this large arts and crafts chain so you can browse in person through a million other paper crafting goodies you never even knew you needed.

Olde English Crackers
(oldenglishcrackers.com)

The only place I've found so far in the United States that sells cracker snaps! And, they have lightning-fast shipping.

Paper Source
(paper-source.com)

A great selection of beautifully colored card stock, handmade papers, bookmaking supplies, and gifts. I spend a lot of time (and money) on their website.

Parcel
(shopparcel.com)

If you can't visit, there's an online version of the brick and mortar store, with tons of vintage wallpapers and other paper and non-paper notions. We purchased many of the props for the photo shoot for this book at Parcel. A visit is like falling down the rabbit hole of paper crafting goodness.

INSPIRATION

Here are a few of my favorite paper blogs and artists to keep the inspiration wheels turning.

Blogs

Once Upon a Fold
(uponafold.com.au)

This little Australian paper shop and blog is filled with paper art and inspiration galore.

Folding Trees
(foldingtrees.com)

Though this blog is (sadly) no longer active, they still have tons of paper tutorials—from jewelry to origami.

CRAFT
(blog.craftzine.com)

The mother of all craft blogs, *Craft* covers every kind of DIY, with lots of paper projects represented.

Paper Forest
(paperforest.blogspot.com)

It's easy to get lost in this virtual wonderland of paper art, toys, and DIY.

Of Paper and Things
(ofpaperandthings.blogspot.com)

Paper art and installations (plus a few other things) from around the world.

Paper Artists to Search Online

Su Blackwell
Peter Callesen
Brian Dettmer
Tara Donovan
Anna-Wili Highfield
Elsa Mora
Rob Ryan
Justine Smith
Polly Verity

❖

No Fancy Books Were Harmed in the Making of This Craft Book

I know this is going to come up, so let's not beat around the bush: There are people who believe that no books, under any circumstances, should be destroyed for the sake of art or craft. The books that were upcycled in working on this book were old, picked up from thrift stores, often a bit torn, dog-eared, yellowed, and sometimes moldy with age. I don't believe in ripping up a first-edition copy of *On the Road*, and you *definitely* will not see that here. But I do believe in giving otherwise trashed books a new life—and that's the spirit with which I choose my materials.

Cardboard Curio Shelf, page 38

Book 'Em Wall Pocket, page 19

CHAPTER
· ·

three

THE PAPER HOME

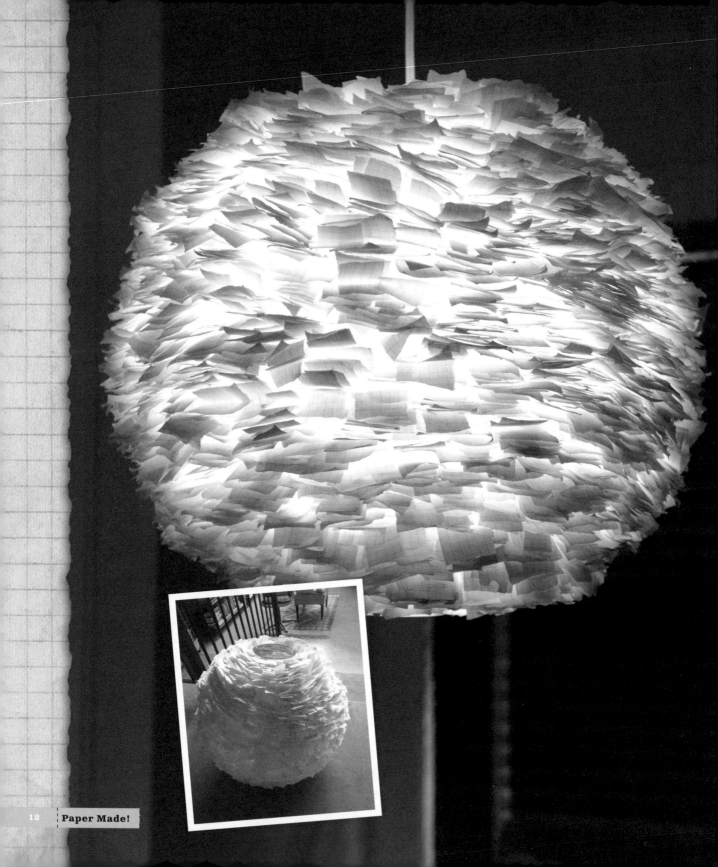

Paper Made!

01 Scrap Happy Globe Lantern

LEVEL ✖✖✖○○

WHAT YOU NEED

• Graph paper, copy paper, or similar (approximately 1 pad of graph paper or ½ ream of copy paper, depending on the dimensions of the lantern)

• White glue

• Small, shallow dish

• Round Chinese paper lantern, any size

• Lightbulb

A few years ago at work, my good friend Courtney and I were tasked with creating a lighting display that cost next to nothing. So we invested in a few rice paper lanterns, gathered a bunch of scrap paper, and went to town. The results were nothing short of stunning. When lit, this lamp looks almost otherworldly, a perfect statement piece for your home that costs very little to create! Admittedly, these lamps take a long time to make, but they require very little concentration—so plan a movie marathon and start gluing. You'll be done before the credits roll on that third rom-com.

1. Rip paper in roughly 2" squares (fig. 1.1). The squares don't have to be perfect—it's even better if they are not.

Fig. 1.1

2. Fold all of these pieces in half (fig. 1.2).

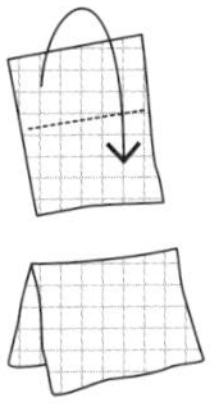

Fig. 1.2

3. Pour the white glue into a shallow dish. Dip the folded edge of one paper square in the glue and gently press it horizontally onto the side of the lantern

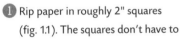

at its midpoint. Repeat with a second square, placing this one just below the first. Continue, working your way down to the bottom of the lantern, then return to the first square and work up to the top (fig. 1.3). The glue will dry quickly so you can work continuously.

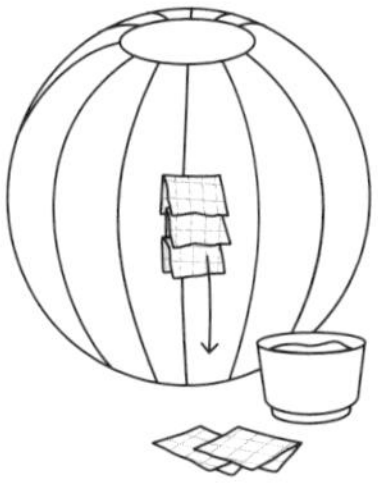

Fig. 1.3

4. Continue adding pieces, working in columns, around the lantern, until you have covered the entire lantern surface (fig. 1.4).

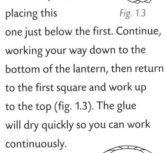

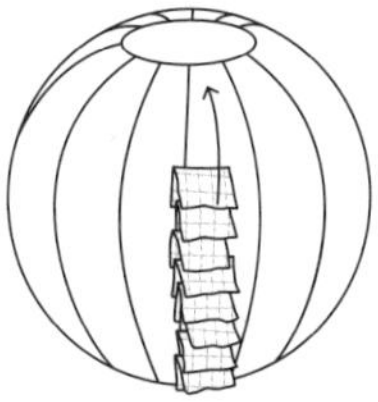

Fig. 1.4

5. Hold up the lantern to a light source to see if you have missed any areas, and repeat step 3 as necessary. Let dry.

6. Add a lightbulb and hang the lantern according to the packaging instructions (fig. 1.6).

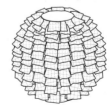

Fig. 1.6

02 | **Songbird Votive**

LEVEL ✕✕✕✕✕

These votive candleholders look lovely just sitting on a table, but wait until you light a candle in them: Tissue paper practically glows in candlelight! There are many papery layers in these votive holders; feel free to add or subtract design elements as you desire. Move the flowers in different patterns, add a few more birds—it's all up to you.

1. Measure the height of the glass votive candleholder and cut a strip of tissue paper to that measurement. Wrap the tissue paper around the votive, overlapping the edges ½", and mark a cut line (fig. 2.1). Remove the tissue and trim it to size.

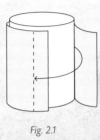

Fig. 2.1

2. Brush the outer surface of the votive (minus the bottom) with decoupage medium and carefully smooth the tissue paper over it (fig. 2.2).

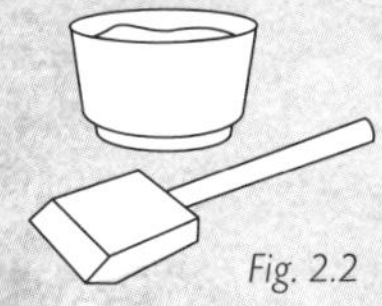

Fig. 2.2

3. Print the flower and bird templates. Place a sheet of tissue paper over the templates and trace them with a pencil (fig. 2.3). Start with the larger pieces like the birds and bigger flowers, and then trace the small details.

Fig. 2.3

4. Use a pair of scissors to cut out all the pieces you traced in step 3.

5. Starting with the larger pieces, brush decoupage medium onto the back of each design and add it to the votive candleholder (fig. 2.5).

Fig. 2.5

6. Brush the decoupage medium over the outer sides of the votive, then let dry.

❁

Paper Cuts

When most of us look at a sheet of paper, we see, well, a sheet of paper. Artist Peter Callesen (petercallesen.com) sees a rowboat floating on the waves, a man climbing a mountain, even the Tower of Babel. Callesen turns ordinary, two-dimensional sheets of paper into fantastical scenes with just a few (okay, lots and *lots* of) tiny cuts.

- *Ruler*
- *Round glass votive candleholder, about 4" diameter*
- *Tissue paper in a variety of colors*
- *Pencil*
- *Scissors*
- *Foam brush*
- *Decoupage medium*
- *Access to a computer with a printer and paper*
- *Flower and bird templates**
- *Water*

* Download at workman.com/papermade

03 | # Prizewinning Bowl

LEVEL ⊗⊗⊗⊗⊗

Chances are you know at least one parent who once upon a time enthusiastically overestimated the number of raffle tickets for a school carnival or community fund-raiser. And if you happen to have access to that parent's basement, you will very likely be able to scavenge an abandoned raffle roll perfect for making a nice centerpiece. Both dimensional and useful, this bowl is—ahem—just the ticket!

WHAT YOU NEED

- Roll of raffle tickets
- Hot glue gun and glue
- Pencil
- Scrap of noncorrugated cardboard
- Scissors
- Foam brush
- Decoupage medium

1 Carefully remove the tape from the outside of the raffle ticket roll. Apply a small dot of hot glue to the wrong side of the last ticket in the roll and press it against the rest of the roll (fig. 3.1).

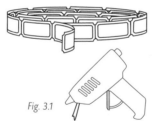

Fig. 3.1

2 Holding the outer edges of the roll in your hands (like a steering wheel), use your thumbs to slowly push the center of the roll down to form a bowl. Adjust the shape of the bowl by pushing down on different parts of the ticket roll. If you push too far, gently press parts of the ticket roll back up (fig. 3.2).

Fig. 3.2

3 Trace the bottom of the bowl onto a piece of cardboard and cut it out (fig. 3.3).

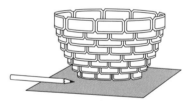

Fig. 3.3

4 Squeeze hot glue over the cardboard circle, and quickly center and stick it to the bottom of the bowl (fig. 3.4).

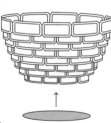

Fig. 3.4

5 Using a foam brush, brush a light layer of decoupage medium over the inside and outside of the bowl. Let dry. Flip the bowl over and brush the bottom of the bowl. Let dry and then brush one more layer over the entire bowl. Let dry once more before using.

04 | Book 'Em Wall Pocket

LEVEL ✪✪✪✪○

Since I don't anticipate having the luxury of a foyer anytime soon, I usually collect my incoming and outgoing mail in some sort of wall receptacle. It's so hard to find one that looks good *and* works, but, as it turns out, old books make really fantastic (and really attractive) wall organizers. You can make them in all sorts of sizes, depending on your wall, your organizing needs, and the size of the books you find in the giveaway bin.

WHAT YOU NEED

• *Craft knife*

• *Self-healing cutting mat*

• *Hardcover book that's past its prime*

• *Ruler*

• *Decorative paper to line the inside of the mail holder*

• *Pencil*

• *Hot glue gun and glue*

• *Lightweight cardboard from food packaging (cracker or cereal boxes work well)*

• *4" of 1"-wide cotton twill tape or ribbon*

1 Use the craft knife and cutting mat to carefully separate the cover of the book from the pages. Tear out four book pages and set aside the rest of the book for another project (such as the Paperback Riser, page 234).

2 Lay the book cover flat, right side down. Measure the length and width of the cover and cut a piece of decorative paper to match (to use as the lining). Set aside.

3 Lay one of the book pages flat. On top of it, stand up the book cover so that the spine faces away from you. With the back cover straight, fold out the front cover at approximately a 45-degree angle (fig. 4.3). With a pencil, trace around the inside of the cover onto the book page. Draw a straight line connecting the open ends to form a triangular shape.

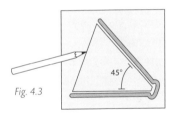

Fig. 4.3

4 Add ½" to all sides except for the last line you drew (fig. 4.4). Cut out the shape, and don't erase the pencil lines.

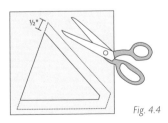

Fig. 4.4

5 With the pencil lines faceup (so they remain visible), hot glue the paper shape to a piece of cardboard. Trim off the excess cardboard around the paper (fig. 4.5).

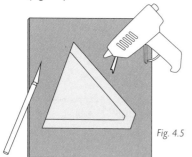

Fig. 4.5

6 Squeeze hot glue onto the other side of the cardboard piece and press it onto a second book page (fig. 4.6). Trim off the excess paper.

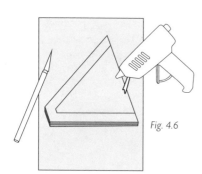

Fig. 4.6

7 Use a craft knife to gently score along the traced pencil lines, and bend the edges up at the score lines to make tabs. Make three to four ½" cuts into the rounded corner to ease the fold as you bend the tabs. This is one side panel (fig. 4.7).

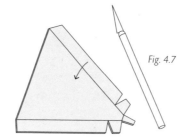

Fig. 4.7

8 Repeat steps 4 through 7 to make the second side panel.

9 Hot glue the outside of the tabs on one edge of one side panel to the inside edge of the book cover. Repeat for the other panel on the opposite edge (fig 4.9).

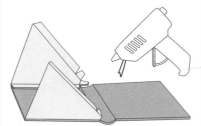

Fig. 4.9

10 Hot glue the remaining tabs on each panel to the matching edges of the book cover.

11 Fold the twill tape or ribbon in half and hot glue the ends to the center inside edge of the back cover (fig. 4.11).

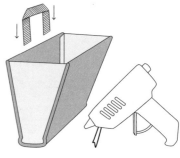

Fig. 4.11

12 Hot glue the decorative paper lining inside the book cover, covering the ends of the twill tape and the tabs of the side panels (fig. 4.12).

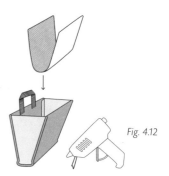

Fig. 4.12

05 | Ring Around the Rosy Vase

LEVEL ⊗ ⊗ ⊗ ⊗ ⊘

One of the best techniques for turning humble materials into something spectacular is through the use of repetition (for more evidence of this, see the Scrap Happy Globe Lantern, page 12, or the Paper's on a Roll Frame, page 42). One rolled strip of magazine isn't so special but dozens, stacked up to cover a simple glass vessel, make it spectacular. This is one of those *aha!* projects: People won't be able to tell what this vase is made from at first, but their oohs and ahhs will only increase when they discover the secret!

(see the Scrap Happy Globe Lantern, page 12, or the Paper's on a Roll Frame, page 42)

WHAT YOU NEED

- *Magazine or catalog*
- *Craft knife*
- *Ruler*
- *Self-healing cutting mat*
- *Round implements of different sizes for rolling (a pencil, thin marker, and wide marker work well)*
- *Small brush*
- *White glue*
- *Decoupage medium*
- *Pencil*
- *Glass jar (clean peanut butter or jelly jars from the recycling bin work well)*
- *Noncorrugated cardboard circle (at least 1" wider than the circumference of the jar)*

---

① Tear out a handful of sheets of magazine pages. Use the craft knife, ruler, and cutting mat to cut ¼" strips down the length of the magazine (fig. 5.1). Cut about 600 strips in total. *Note:* If cutting gets tedious, continue with steps 2 and 3 for a spell and then return to step 1.

② Select a paper strip and choose a cylindrical object to use as a rolling instrument. Starting at one end of the paper strip, roll the paper around the object once, then brush some glue on the next section of the strip and roll again. Continue rolling, adding glue at each rotation, until you reach the end of the paper strip (fig. 5.2).

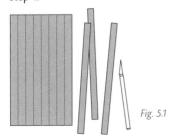

Fig. 5.1

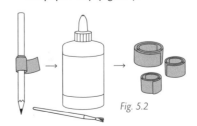

Fig. 5.2

3 Dab glue at the end of the strip to seal the coil. *Optional:* To make a thicker roll, once you reach the end of a strip, attach another magazine strip there and roll it around the first. Repeat for an even thicker roll.

4 Repeat steps 2 and 3 with the remaining strips and various rolling instruments to create coils of different sizes. Then, brush each roll with decoupage medium and set them aside to dry.

5 Use the pencil to trace the bottom of the jar onto the cardboard, add 1" to the diameter, and use the craft knife to cut it out. Then measure and cut a magazine page in a circle 2" larger in diameter than the base (fig. 5.5).

Fig. 5.5

6 Brush one side of the cardboard circle with white glue and center and press it facedown onto the magazine circle. Use the craft knife to cut slits 1" apart from the edge of the magazine circle to the edge of the cardboard circle (fig. 5.6).

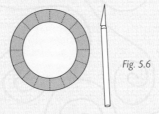

Fig. 5.6

7 Brush the edges of the magazine circle with glue and wrap each 1" tab around the edge of the cardboard circle.

8 Brush glue along the outer edge of the circle and attach a row of paper coils around the base. Vary the size of the coils, making sure that the edges of each coil touch the next (fig. 5.8).

Fig. 5.8

9 Continue to glue the paper coils, stacking them in uneven rows. Every three rows, brush the inside and outside of the vase with decoupage medium and let dry. Leave more space between the coils as the rows stack higher.

10 Check the height of the vase by placing the jar inside it. Add paper coils until they rise about 1" above the glass jar (fig. 5.10).

11 Remove the jar. Brush the inside and outside of the vase with decoupage medium and let it dry completely before replacing the jar (fig. 5.11).

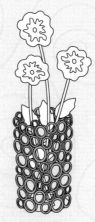

Fig. 5.10–11

Two Types of Stripes Switch Plates

WHAT YOU NEED

- *Scraps of tissue paper in different colors or scraps of different kinds of paper from magazines, newspapers, origami paper, or wallpaper*

- *Ruler*

- *Craft knife*

- *Self-healing cutting mat*

- *Foam brushes*

- *Decoupage medium*

- *Sheet of card stock 1" larger than the switch plate on all sides*

- *2 switch plates*

- *Pencil*

- *White glue*

LEVEL ⊗⊗⊗⊗⊗

I'm a stripe-loving girl. Thick or thin, vertical or horizontal, I'll take them all. These two switch plate covers have the same color story but are made with two different techniques and result in two totally different looks. You can choose one or, assuming you have more than one light switch to decorate, make them both!

① *To make tissue paper strips:* Tear tissue paper into approximately ten ½" × 2" strips. Don't worry that they aren't perfect strips—irregular looks better!

To make scrap paper strips: Using a ruler, craft knife, and cutting mat, cut approximately ten ¼" × 2" strips of scrap paper.

② *For tissue paper strips:* Brush a small amount of decoupage medium across the width of the card stock and attach tissue paper strips individually to cover the whole sheet (fig. 6.2). Let dry for one hour. *Note:* You can layer strips on top of each other; just allow the first strip to dry before you add another layer.

Fig. 6.2

For scrap paper strips: Lightly brush decoupage medium over the back of each strip and apply them one at a time to the card stock, from top to bottom, overlapping the strips. Let dry for one hour.

3 Lay the card stock piece right side down on a cutting mat and trim the strips around the edges (fig. 6.3). Center the switch plate right side down on top of the card stock.

Fig. 6.3

4 Trace around the switch plate with a pencil. Set aside the switch plate and use the craft knife to miter each corner at a 45-degree angle (fig. 6.4). Remove the triangles of paper.

Fig. 6.4

5 Brush white glue on the right side of the switch plate, flip it over, and center it back on the paper, with the switch plate wrong side up.

6 Fold the side edges of the paper to the back of the switch plate, then the top and bottom edges (fig. 6.6). Press to adhere.

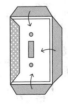

Fig. 6.6

7 Cut an X in the center of the paper cover and fold the paper edges over to the back of the switch plate (fig. 6.7). Press to adhere.

Fig. 6.7

07 | **Bird on a Wire Mobile**

LEVEL ⊗ ⊗ ⊗ ⊗ ⊗

O ld maps are a wonderful found material to work with. They're colorful and graphic and also add personality to a project. Maps remind us of travel, adventure, time on the open road—feeling free as a bird. For this mobile, choose a map that speaks to you. A street map of your childhood town would be perfect in your child's nursery, a nautical map of the ocean is a great match for a beach house, and a road map from your cross-country trip with your college friend would make a very special gift.

WHAT YOU NEED

- *Access to a computer with a printer and paper*
- *Bird body, wing, and tail templates **
- *White paper*
- *Craft knife*
- *Self-healing cutting mat*
- *Small foam brush*
- *White glue*
- *Noncorrugated cardboard (from cereal or other food packaging)*
- *Old maps*
- *Pencil*
- *Hot glue gun and glue*
- *¼" circle hole punch*
- *Scissors*
- *String or twine*
- *Branch or piece of driftwood*

* Download at workman.com/papermade

1. Print the bird body, wing, and tail templates and cut them out using the craft knife and cutting mat.

2. Lay the maps flat and brush one side of the noncorrugated cardboard with white glue. Press the cardboard onto the map and let it dry. Then spread glue on the opposite side and press it onto the map, so the cardboard is covered on both sides (fig. 7.2). Let dry.

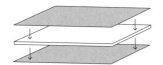

Fig. 7.2

3. Use the templates to trace four bird bodies, eight wings, and four tails onto the maps. Transfer the dots onto the bird bodies to use as guidelines for providing holes in step 5. Cut out the templates, making sure to cut the slit in the bird body.

4. To assemble the bird, slide the tail into the slit in the back of the bird body. Hot glue the wings in place on either side of the bird (fig. 7.4). Gently fold the wings so that they stick out. Repeat with the remaining three birds.

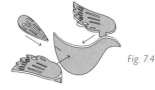

Fig. 7.4

5. Use the hole punch to make holes at each marked dot on the bird bodies (fig. 7.5). Cut twelve 2' lengths of string or twine and thread and tie one end of each in an overhand knot at each hole.

Fig. 7.5

6. Tie the three loose ends from each bird together 3" above each bird. Then loop each bundle of strings around a branch or piece of driftwood and knot.

7. Cut two 2' lengths of string or twine. Loop one end of one string around the left side of the branch about 2" in from the edge of the wood and make an overhand knot. Repeat for the right side. Bring the two ends together, leveling the wood between them, and tie in an overhand knot (fig. 7.7).

Fig. 7.7

VARIATION

If you want a more colorful mobile, make your birds with magazine scraps and construction paper. Think birds are for the birds? How about fish, flowers, or trees?

The Paper Home 27

Pulp Fiction Bowls

LEVEL ⊗ ⊗ ⊗ ⊗ ⊗

WHAT YOU NEED

(makes 3 stacking bowls)

- Old newspaper or paper shopping bag
- 3 round, medium-size balloons
- 3 bowls with rounded bottoms, about the size of an inflated balloon
- Small plastic container (like a 6" × 8" rectangular take-out container)
- Wallpaper paste
- Water
- Paperback book
- Scissors
- Tissue paper (optional)

I had the idea for these bowls when my husband decided to do a major purge of some of his trashier (and trashed) fantasy and sci-fi novels. I have always loved the look and feel of papier-mâché bowls—they are at once sturdy and light as a feather—and was looking for a new material to experiment with. These paperbacks turned out to be perfect: You can read bits and pieces of the book as you look at the bowl! And though no one will accuse you of cutting up one of the classics, you *will* get your hands a little dirty with this one, so just roll with it.

1 Protect your work surface by laying down some old newspaper or a paper shopping bag.

2 Inflate the balloons to three slightly different sizes, as desired. Prop each balloon in a bowl, knot at the bottom. (This will stabilize the balloon while you are papier-mâchéing.) In the plastic container, mix two parts wallpaper paste to one part water.

3 Tear out pages of the book in chunks and then tear the pages into approximately ½"-wide strips (rip the pages widthwise, parallel to the written lines on the page—they'll tear easier and you can read a sentence here and there!) (fig. 8.3).

Fig. 8.3

4 Dip each strip in the wallpaper paste, coating it evenly on both sides. Lay the first strip on the top of the balloon, with one end

in the center and the rest of the strip down the side. Continue applying strips, making sure each strip lies flat against the balloon, so they appear to radiate out of the center top of the balloon (fig. 8.4). Set aside to dry and start on the remaining balloons.

Fig. 8.4

5 Return to the first balloon and apply another layer of strips. Repeat on each balloon until you have four layers of strips. Let dry overnight.

6 Gently deflate each balloon by snipping a tiny bit of the balloon with scissors. The bowls might start to cave slightly as the balloon deflates, but they will retain their shape.

Optional: Tear strips of colored tissue paper and papier-mâché them to the inside of the bowls with the wallpaper paste (fig. 8.6). Let dry completely.

Fig. 8.6

09 | Silence of the Alarms Clock

LEVEL ⊗ ⊗ ⊗ ⊗ ⊗

While there's nothing funny about a really loud alarm clock, there's something rather satisfying about one that cannot make a sound. There it sits, ever so silently, simply telling time. Take that, Monday morning!

WHAT YOU NEED

- Access to a computer with a printer and paper
- Alarm clock templates*
- Craft knife
- Self-healing cutting mat
- Painter's tape
- Foam core or corrugated cardboard
- Pencil
- Scraps of wallpaper or other vintage papers in various patterns
- Foam brush
- White glue
- Ruler
- Hammer and a nail or a drill fitted with a ¼" boring bit
- Clock kit (sample is from klockit.com)
- Hot glue gun and glue

* Download at workman.com/papermade

1. Print out the alarm clock templates and cut them out with a craft knife and cutting mat.

2. Tape the templates to foam core or corrugated paper and trace them with a pencil. Trace the half circles twice to make one smaller and one larger circle. Remove the templates and cut along the traced lines (fig. 9.2).

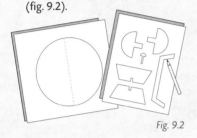

Fig. 9.2

3. Choose the patterned papers you want for each piece of the clock. Brush one side of each of the clock pieces with white glue and affix the papers to each piece. Let dry and cut off the excess paper with the craft knife (fig. 9.3).

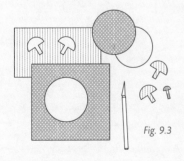

Fig. 9.3

4. Repeat step 3 for the other sides of the clock pieces.

5. Measure and mark a dot at the very center of the small and large circles (fig. 9.5).

Fig. 9.5

6. Using the dot as your guide, hammer or drill a hole in the center of both circles (fig. 9.6).

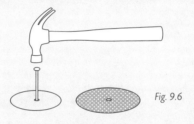

Fig. 9.6

7. Follow the manufacturer's instructions to assemble the clock kit (fig. 9.7).

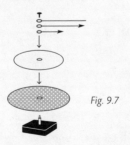

Fig. 9.7

8. Hot glue the bells, handle, and hammer behind the large circle (fig. 9.8).

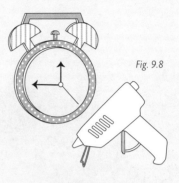

Fig. 9.8

9. Insert the bottom of the large circle into the slats on the base of the clock to stand the clock upright (fig. 9.9).

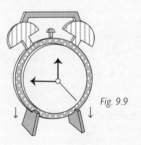

Fig. 9.9

WHAT YOU NEED
....

- Double-wide ticket rolls
  in two colors

- Painter's tape

- Clear contact paper

- Ruler

- Craft knife

- Self-healing cutting mat

- Access to a sewing
  machine and contrasting
  thread (optional)

10 | One-Way Ticket Place Mat

LEVEL ● ● ○ ○ ○

I have recently officially added raffle ticket rolls to my ever-growing roster of incredibly-versatile-found-papers-to-make-things-with. This project is just the ticket for crafting with little ones—working with strips of raffle tickets is particularly simple because they're already cut perfectly straight and are easy to tear. Plus kids (of all ages) will be proud to use their work and eat their breakfast cereal off these place mats. Talk about a meal ticket!

1. Rip off eight strips of six tickets from one ticket roll. Rip off six strips of eight tickets from the other ticket roll.

2. On a clean surface, lay out the longer strips of tickets lengthwise and tape them down along the left edge (fig. 10.2).

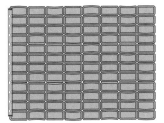

Fig. 10.2

3. Start weaving in the shorter strips. Take one strip and weave under and over until you reach the opposite edge. Push the short strip close to the taped edge (fig. 10.3).

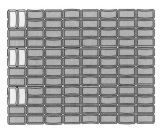

Fig. 10.3

4. Weave the next strip over, then under, until you reach the opposite edge. Push this strip as close as you can to the first strip (fig. 10.4).

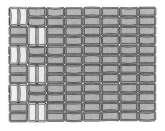

Fig. 10.4

5. Continue weaving the short strips until you reach the end of the long strips. Your place mat should be six strips high by eight strips across.

6. Roll out a piece of clear contact paper and remove the paper backing. Carefully press the back of the woven tickets to the contact paper.

7. Leaving a ¼" allowance on all sides, cut around the contact paper with a craft knife on a cutting mat (fig. 10.7).

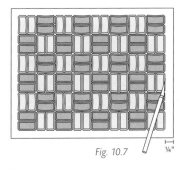

Fig. 10.7   ¼"

8. Roll out a second piece of clear contact paper and remove the paper backing. Flip the woven mat and carefully press it against the contact paper, making sure the contact paper seals together at the edge. Leaving a ¼" allowance, trim around the contact paper to line up with the first side. *Optional:* Stitch around the place mat with a ¼" seam allowance.

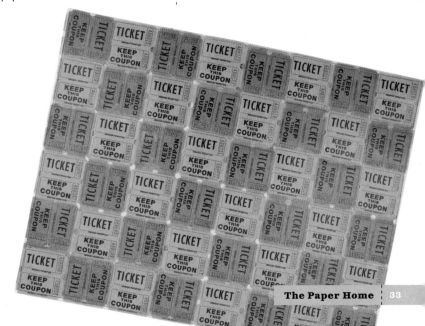

Strike Your Fancy Matchbox

LEVEL ✪ ✪ ✪ ✪ ✪

WHAT YOU NEED

- Scraps of paper (at least 2" × 8")
- Small matchbox
- Pencil
- Craft knife
- Self-healing cutting mat
- Foam brush
- White glue
- Small scraps of paper and computer, typewriter, or pen (optional)

A paper-covered matchbox is perfectly paired with a fancy candle or votive candleholder at gift time. Type a secret message—say, "a match made in heaven," "my perfect match," "light my fire," or "you strike me as perfect"—and hide it inside the matchbox. They're such a simple little luxury and an absolute cinch to make—just remember to grab a few freebie matchboxes every time you go out to eat and you'll be set for your next sweet DIY gift.

1 Lay a piece of paper right side down, place a matchbox on it, and trace around the matchbox. Without shifting the box, lift it up on its side and trace it again before flipping it down to trace the third surface. You should have a long rectangle exactly the width of the matchbox and the length of three sides combined (fig. 11.1).

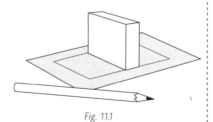

Fig. 11.1

2 Use the craft knife and cutting mat to cut out the rectangle (fig. 11.2).

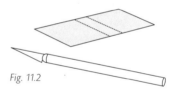

Fig. 11.2

strike while it's hot

light my fire

you strike me as perfect

a match made in heaven

light my fire

All Fired Up

In 1507, the Aztec emperor Montezuma prepared his empire for the New Fire Ceremony, a ritual of renewed life that took place every 52 years. Supplies collected for tribute to the gods included things like feather clothing, obsidian knives and arrows, bronze axes, and rolls and rolls of paper. The collected paper—nearly a half million sheets—was folded, rolled up in bundles, and tipped with rubber and incense for burning.

3 Brush glue onto the wrong side of the paper rectangle and press it to the bottom of the matchbox (fig. 11.3). Fold the paper around the matchbox, avoiding the striking surface on one side and creasing the paper at the edges.

4 Trim off any excess paper and let dry. Repeat to make a set of matchboxes. *Optional:* Use a pencil, pen, computer, or typewriter to write little notes on scrap paper. Cut these into strips to fit into the matchbox (fig. 11.4).

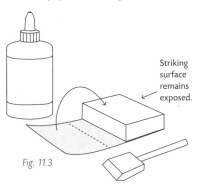

Striking surface remains exposed.

Fig. 11.3

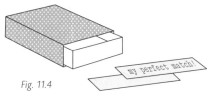

my perfect match!

Fig. 11.4

match made in heaven

my perfect match

12 Painterly Frame

LEVEL ✪✪✪✪✪

Ah, paint chips, how I love thee! Every time I go into a home improvement store, I can't help myself. I have to swing by the paint section and stare at the paint chips. Any DIY decorator worth her salt has a box of paint chips for future projects, but paint chips are a pretty transformative decorating material themselves. Even if you never get around to painting the kitchen that perfect shade of green, you can still use those green paint chips to completely overhaul an oh-so-basic picture frame. These frames look best in groups, so grab your paint chip stash (you know you have one) and get to work.

---

1 Brush one panel of the front of the frame with decoupage medium. Select a paint chip and line up one of its edges with the inside edge of the frame. Press it flat into the glue and let dry for a few minutes (fig. 12.1).

Fig. 12.1

2 Lay the frame front side down on a cutting mat. Use the craft knife to cut off the excess paint chips (fig. 12.2).

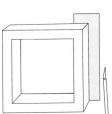

Fig. 12.2

3 Repeat for the other three front panels.

4 Repeat steps 1 and 2 to cover the four sides of the frame (fig. 12.4).

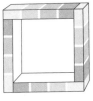

Fig. 12.4

5 Allow frame to dry, and use the foam brush to give the paint chips three coats of decoupage medium, allowing the frame to dry completely between coats.

WHAT YOU NEED

- *Shadow box–style frame (6" × 6")*
- *Foam brush*
- *Decoupage medium*
- *6 to 8 paint chips (at least as long and as wide as the frame)*
- *Craft knife*
- *Self-healing cutting mat*

Cardboard Curio Shelf

LEVEL ✪✪✪✕✕

WHAT YOU NEED
....

- Drafting or drawing compass
- Pencil
- Corrugated cardboard; 2 or 3 book boxes (12" × 12" × 8") should do
- Craft knife
- Self-healing cutting mat
- Ruler
- Wood glue
- C-clamps
- Superglue
- Binder clips

Curio shelves are perfect little spots to display a favorite object or tiny collection. They're usually made from wood, but those humble sheets of corrugated cardboard, when layered, can be just as sturdy. In this project, the design of the cardboard is celebrated, not just its function. And speaking of humble materials, I got inspired by some other office supplies lying around, so instead of the usual hanging hardware, this shelf is hung with good old binder clips.

1. Use the compass to trace six 12"-diameter half circles on the cardboard, making sure that the cardboard is oriented so that the diameter runs perpendicular to the corrugation. Use a craft knife and cutting mat to cut out the half circles (fig. 13.1).

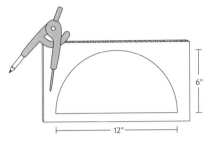

Fig. 13.1

2. Use the compass to draw and cut eleven more half circles, reducing each one in size by 1" in diameter.

3. Stack and glue the six 12" half circles together, lining up all the edges.

4. Squeeze wood glue across one side of the 11" half circle and center it along the straight edge of one of the 12" half circles (fig. 13.4).

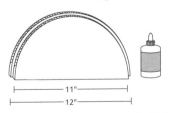

Fig. 13.4

5. To create the shelf, repeat step 4 and adhere each subsequent half circle to the previous one (fig. 13.5). Let dry.

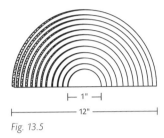

Fig. 13.5

6. Lay the shelf on a piece of cardboard, arced edges up, and trace around the shelf to get a trapezoid shape, as shown. Add ½" to the shape at the top of the shelf. (fig. 13.6).

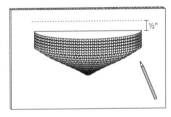

Fig. 13.6

7. Use a ruler to straighten the traced lines, and cut out the shape to make the backing.

8. Squeeze wood glue across one side of the backing and press the flat side of the shelf onto it, making sure that the ½" allowance of the backing remains at the top of the shelf. Clamp these pieces together and let dry.

9. Spread superglue on the inside of one binder clip and clip it to the top of the backing, 1" in from the side. Repeat with the second binder clip, 1" in from the opposite side (fig. 13.9). Let dry, then hang as desired.

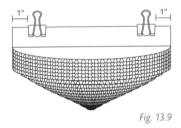

Fig. 13.9

❖

Chair Apparent

We've all been known in our college days to use an old cardboard box as impromptu furniture, but Frank Gehry raised cardboard furniture to an art form. His Wiggle Chair (1972), consisting of sixty layers of cardboard held together by screws, is still made and sold by Vitra, can hold thousands of pounds, and has won countless design awards.

14 | **Family Portraits**

LEVEL ⊗ ⊗ ⊗ ⊗ ⊗

WHAT YOU NEED

- *Digital family photos*
- *Access to a computer with a printer and paper*
- *Tracing paper*
- *Pencil*
- *Craft knife*
- *Self-healing cutting mat*
- *Glue stick*
- *Card stock*
- *Larger piece of paper (at least the size of the original photo) for the background*
- *Scraps of various papers*

Silhouette cutting started in the 17th century, when lords and ladies hired artists to create elaborate likenesses of the royal class. So much has changed. Today we have photography to record our family memories, and you don't have to be royal to get your own silhouette cut—you can do it yourself! These paper silhouettes are the picture-perfect way to blend art and family memories, and you can customize the silhouettes to match your decor. When's the last time you got your family to do that?!

1 Select a digital photo to silhouette. Choose one that has a fairly simple composition and is easy to trace. Enlarge it to the desired size on a computer, print it, and layer a sheet of tracing paper over the photo (fig. 14.1).

Fig. 14.1

2 Trace the full silhouette. Then choose the details you want to feature (such as figures, their clothes, shoes, a pet) and trace them individually (fig. 14.2). *Note:* Make sure all of your tracings are closed shapes that can be cut out easily.

Fig. 14.2

3 Cut out the main silhouette and the details (fig. 14.3).

Fig. 14.3

4 Glue each tracing onto a piece of card stock to give it structure, and let dry. Cut them out.

5 Select a paper for the main silhouette, trace around the template onto the front of the paper, and then cut it out with a craft knife. Glue it to the background paper (fig. 14.5).

Fig. 14.5

6 Repeat step 5 for all of the details, and glue them to the silhouette (fig. 14.6). Repeat from step 1 to create additional portraits. *Optional:* Draw in any other details of the silhouette with a pencil.

Fig. 14.6

15 | Paper's on a Roll Frame

Do you get a lot of catalogs that you don't really want? I do. I've signed up for every single "please don't send me any more catalogs" list, and yet every time I open my mailbox, there they are. Sure, you can recycle them, but making them into something you can actually use is even better. Impress your next dinner guests by decorating your walls with frames like this—made entirely from paper found in the recycling bin!

* * *

WHAT YOU NEED

- *Catalog*
- *Ruler*
- *Pencil*
- *Craft knife*
- *Self-healing cutting mat*
- *Foam brush*
- *White glue*
- *Noncorrugated cardboard, enough for a 10" and a 6½" square*
- *Wood glue*

1 Tear out catalog pages and cut them lengthwise (top to bottom of the page) into ninety-six 3½"-wide strips.

2 Take one strip and wrap the end around the pencil (fig. 15.2). Brush a small bit of white glue onto the paper and roll again, securing the paper to itself.

Fig. 15.2

3 Tightly roll the paper toward the opposite end, applying a small amount of glue every two or three rolls to secure. At the end, brush glue onto the tip of the strip and press it to the roll to seal it.

4 Repeat steps 2 and 3 to make ninety-five more rolls. Set them aside.

5 Use the craft knife to cut one 10" square and one 6½" square from the noncorrugated cardboard (fig. 15.5).

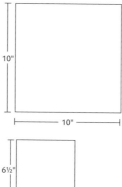

Fig. 15.5

6 Use a ruler and pencil to measure and mark a 4" square in the center of the 10" square. Use the craft knife to cut out the 4" square to make the frame (fig. 15.6).

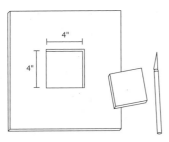

Fig. 15.6

7 To cover the frame, cut an 11" square sheet of paper from the catalog. *Note:* You may need to piece two or more catalog pages together to make this sheet.

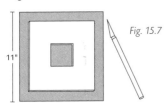

Fig. 15.7

8 Brush one side of the frame with white glue, and center and press it onto the catalog sheet (fig. 15.8).

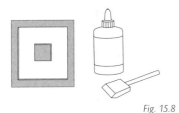

Fig. 15.8

9 Use the craft knife to miter each corner of the sheet at a 45-degree angle and remove the triangles of paper. Then cut an X into the paper at the center of the frame (fig. 15.9).

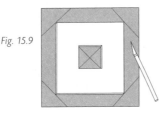

Fig. 15.9

10 Brush the visible edges of the catalog square with glue. Fold the paper around the edge of the cardboard, and press to stick (fig. 15.10).

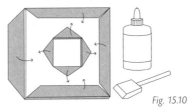

Fig. 15.10

11 Cut a 10" square sheet of paper from the catalog (again, you may need to piece two or more pages together). Cut out a 4" square from the middle, as in step 6. Brush the back of the frame with white glue, and center and press it onto the paper sheet (fig. 15.11). Let dry.

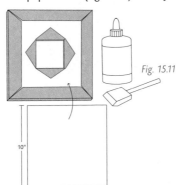

Fig. 15.11

12 Cut out two 6½" square sheets of catalog. Brush the 6½" cardboard square with glue, one side at a time, and center and press the sheets onto the square to cover it. Let dry.

13 Squeeze a line of wood glue along three edges of one side of the square (fig. 15.13). Center and press it onto the back of the frame. (This is the pocket where a photo or small print will slide into the frame.) Let dry.

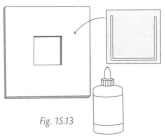

Fig. 15.13

14 Squeeze a thin line of white glue along the seam of one of the rolls from step 2 and attach it horizontally to the top left front of the frame. Repeat, working clockwise around the frame horizontally and vertically (fig. 15.14).

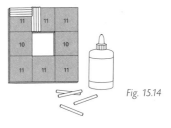

Fig. 15.14

16 | **Give Me an E! Letter**

LEVEL ⊗ ⊗ ⊗ ⊗ ⊗

T he design world is having a big-time love affair with salvaged letters. Scavenged from old signs and billboards, these letters are a great alternative to framed art on a wall. But since they've gotten so popular, they have also become seriously pricey. These papier-mâché letters—made from cardboard, paper scraps, and glue—are scandalously cheap to make.

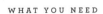
(makes 1 letter)

- *Black permanent marker or access to a printer and photocopier*
- *Large cardboard box*
- *Craft knife*
- *Self-healing cutting mat*
- *Ruler*
- *Pieces of lighter, non-corrugated cardboard (a priority mail envelope or food packaging works well)*
- *Hot glue gun and glue*
- *Paper scraps (old crossword puzzles and comics are great)*
- *Bowl*
- *Water*
- *White glue*
- *Foam brush*
- *Brush-on sealer or varnish*

❶ Determine the size letter and the typeface you would like to use. Either draw the outline of the letter freehand with the marker on the side of a flattened cardboard box or use a photocopier to enlarge and print a letter sample you like and trace it onto the box. For some inspiration, search online for old signage letters.

❷ Use the craft knife and a cutting mat to cut out the letter (fig. 16.2). Then trace and cut out a second letter, using the first as a template.

❸ Cut 3"-wide strips of the thinner cardboard to make the sides of the letters (fig. 16.3). (The number of strips of cardboard will vary according to the size and surface area of the letter.)

Fig. 16.3

❹ Align the long edge of one strip against the outer edge of one of the cardboard letters. Hot glue it in place along the seam (fig. 16.4). At the end of the strip, overlap a new strip about ½" and glue it in place. Continue attaching strips until the entire perimeter of the letter is covered.

Fig. 16.4

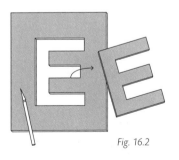

Fig. 16.2

5 Glue the second cardboard letter to the opposite edge of the strips, "closing up" the letter (fig. 16.5).

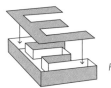

Fig. 16.5

6 Tear 1" strips of paper scraps. Fill a bowl with one part water to two parts glue.

7 One at a time, dip the strips into the bowl of glue, remove some of the excess glue with your fingers, and carefully apply the strips to the surface of the letter (fig. 16.7). Repeat until the entire letter is covered. Let dry completely.

Fig. 16.7

8 Cover the letter with a second layer of paper strips. Apply this layer very carefully so there are no bubbles or creases in the paper. Let dry completely.

9 To finish, paint the letter with two coats of sealer or varnish. Let the letter dry completely after each coat.

WHAT YOU NEED
. . . .

(makes a set of 20 blocks)

- *Access to a computer with a printer and paper*
- *Building block templates**
- *Craft knife*
- *Self-healing cutting mat*
- *Pencil*
- *Corrugated cardboard from 1 box (approximately 18" × 12" × 12")*
- *Foam brush*
- *Decoupage medium*
- *Magazine pages or other paper*

17 | Cardboard Building Blocks

LEVEL ✪ ✪ ✪ ✪ ✪

In 1952, designer Charles Eames created his very own House of Cards, interlocking paper pieces featuring images of what Eames called the "good stuff," pictures of things like "familiar and nostalgic objects from the animal, mineral, and vegetable kingdoms." The building blocks in this project, inspired by Eames, feature my own "good stuff"—familiar and nostalgic objects from fashion magazines—but you can cover them with any paper that strikes your fancy.

1 Print the block templates and cut them out using a craft knife and cutting mat (fig. 17.1).

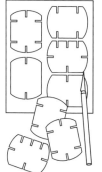

Fig. 17.1

2 Then trace each of the templates four times onto corrugated cardboard and cut out the pieces.

* Download at workman.com/papermade

③ Brush decoupage medium on one side of each block and press them, sticky side down, onto the magazine pages. Let dry, then cut away the excess magazine page with the craft knife (fig. 17.3).

④ Repeat step 3 for the other side of the pieces.

⑤ Brush decoupage medium all over one side of each piece and let dry. Flip over and thoroughly brush medium onto the other side of each piece. Let dry.

⑥ When the pieces are completely dry, start assembling them (fig. 17.6).

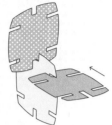

Fig. 17.6

Fig. 17.3

WHAT YOU NEED
. . . .

- *Newspaper*
- *Ruler*
- *Craft knife*
- *Self-healing cutting mat*
- *Binder clips*
- *Needle and gray thread*
- *Medium-size mixing bowl*
- *Plastic wrap*
- *Foam brush*
- *Decoupage medium*

❖

Extra! Extra!

The average American uses seven trees a year in paper, wood, and other products made from trees. This amounts to about 2 billion trees per year. Recycling a single run of the Sunday *New York Times* would save 75,000 trees. Think about how many paper projects you could dream up using an entire Sunday *Times!*

18 | Sunday Paper Bowl

LEVEL ✪ ✪ ✪ ✪ ✪

It's a long-standing tradition in my family to spend Sunday mornings (and sometimes afternoons) curled up on the couch with a cup of tea and *The New York Times.* It's a pretty thick paper, and you know what that means: a heavy load to recycle. But here's a project to lighten that load. Maybe you could get started on your Sunday Paper Bowl on Sunday night.

1 Open the newspaper and select about six full pages. Layer the pages and, using a ruler, craft knife, and cutting mat, cut ½" strips that run lengthwise down the paper. You will need about ninety-nine paper strips to make a 12"-diameter bowl.

2 Select three strips and secure them together at one end with a binder clip. Gently braid the strips together (fig. 18.2).

Fig. 18.2

3 Remove the binder clip and twist the braid at both ends to keep it from unraveling. Then repeat step 2 to make thirty-two more braided pieces.

4 To start the bowl, thread the needle, and tie the ends of the thread in a knot. Select a braided piece, coil one

end tightly against itself, and stitch along the seam. Continue coiling and stitching the braid to itself (fig. 18.4).

Fig. 18.4

5 Line up another braided strip with the end of the first. Spiral it around the base coil and stitch it as you did in step 4 to secure it.

6 Continue to attach fifteen more braids in the same manner, gently tightening the braids as you go to build the bowl up and slightly out from the base (fig. 18.6).

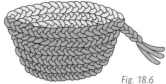

Fig. 18.6

7 Turn the medium-size mixing bowl upside down and cover it with plastic wrap. Fit your newspaper bowl over the inverted bowl and brush one layer of decoupage medium over the outside of the paper bowl. Let dry and remove the paper bowl.

8 Continue to stitch the remaining braided strips along the upper edge of the bowl, building the sides straight up instead of up and out (fig. 18.8).

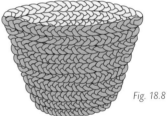

Fig. 18.8

9 Place the finished bowl over the inverted mixing bowl again and brush with another layer of decoupage medium. Let dry and then apply one more coat. Let dry again and remove the newspaper bowl from the mixing bowl.

VARIATION

Trade in your newspaper to make this bowl from postholiday tissue paper, magazines, shredded mail, or other strips of light- or medium-weight paper.

19 | **Paint Chip Mobile**

LEVEL ⊗ ⊗ ⊗ ⊗ ⊗

Mobiles are hanging sculptures of moving parts that twist and sway in the breeze. They can take many forms and be made of pretty much anything. Mobiles are remarkable to look at, but it's also important to consider the way mobiles sound as they move. Paint chips make a very satisfying clicking and clacking in a breeze, almost like hollow bamboo or capiz shells.

WHAT YOU NEED

- Pencil
- Spool of thread, or other item with a traceable 1" circular top
- 30 to 40 paint chips (depending on the size of the chips)
- Scissors
- Access to a sewing machine
- Thread
- String or yarn
- 2 wooden embroidery hoops (one 5" and one 8")
- C-clamp or access to a hook
- Hot glue gun and glue

1 Use a pencil and the spool (or 1" object) to trace 310 circles on the wrong side of the paint chips, and cut them out with scissors. Set aside twenty-two for later, for the top of the mobile (fig. 19.1).

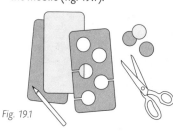

Fig. 19.1

2 Set the sewing machine to straight stitch and select ten to fourteen paint-chip circles to make your first chain. Line up the first two circles ½" apart and feed them through the sewing machine. Before the second circle is stitched, add a third one ½" behind it and continue adding and stitching until you've completed the first chain (fig. 19.2).

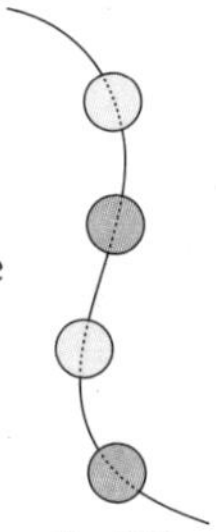

Fig. 19.2

3 Repeat step 2 until twenty more chains, of ten to fourteen circles each, are complete.

4 Lay the chains flat on a clean surface so they don't tangle. Set them aside.

5 Cut four 4" lengths of string or yarn and double knot one end of each equidistant around the large embroidery hoop (fig. 19.5).

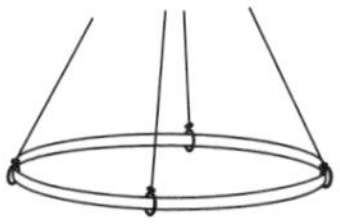

Fig. 19.5

6 Cut four 6" lengths of string or yarn and double knot one end of each equidistant from the others around the smaller embroidery hoop (fig. 19.6). Then gather the untied ends and knot them together.

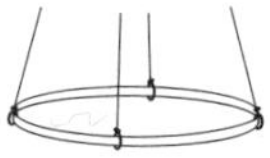

Fig. 19.6

7 Attach a C-clamp to a shelf or window ledge and hang the small hoop from the clamp. Make sure it hangs level; if it doesn't, retie the strings.

8 Holding the large embroidery hoop slightly below the smaller one, match up the four corresponding strings. Tie the ends of the strings on the large embroidery hoop to the loops of string on the smaller hoop (fig. 19.8). Double knot. Make sure the hoops hang level; if they don't, retie the strings.

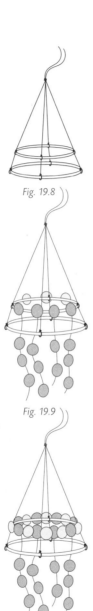

Fig. 19.8

9 Starting on the smaller hoop, hot glue one end of eight paint-chip chains about 1" apart around the outside of the hoop. Some of the wood on the hoop will be visible (fig. 19.9).

Fig. 19.9

10 Retain eight of the circles that you set aside in step 1 and hot glue those to the hoop, concealing the visible areas (fig. 19.10).

11 Moving on to the larger hoop, repeat step 9 with the remaining thirteen paint-chip chains.

12 Repeat step 10 with the remaining thirteen circles you set aside in step 1. Then unclamp the mobile and hang it in a more permanent location.

Fig. 19.10

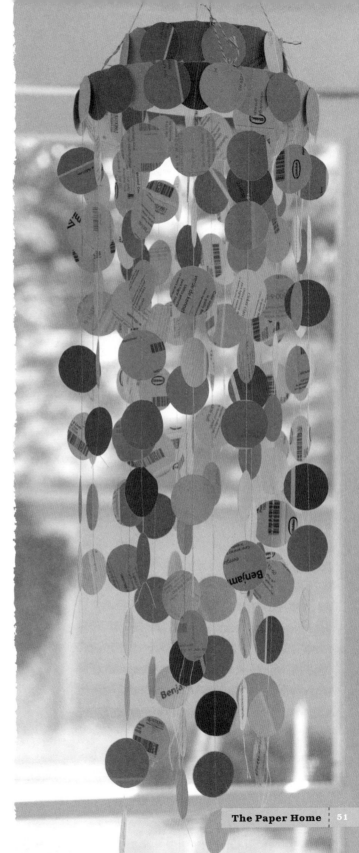

THE 20THCENTURYARTBOOK

COLOR   VICTORIA FINLAY

20 | Book "Shelf"

LEVEL ✪ ✪ ✪ ✪ ✪

As any apartment dweller knows, space for books is always at a premium (as is cash). This shelf keeps your stacks off the floor, costs pennies to make, and doubles as illusion wall art. Your friends will be superimpressed: "How *did* she get those books to hang on the wall?" If you don't have a drill, borrow one from a handy friend or sweet-talk your super.

WHAT YOU NEED
. . . .

- *Hardcover book that's past its prime*

- *Ruler*

- *Pencil*

- *2 L-brackets (size varies based on book size; sample uses 3" brackets for a ¾"-thick book)*

- *Craft knife*

- *Hand drill*

- *Screws (long enough to go through at least three-quarters of the book)*

① Open the back cover of the book. Along the outer edge of the inside cover, use the ruler and pencil to measure and mark 2" from the top and bottom (fig. 20.1) to indicate where the brackets will go.

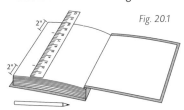

Fig. 20.1

② Center the end of one L-bracket over one of the pencil marks and trace the shape (fig. 20.2). Repeat with the second L-bracket on the second mark.

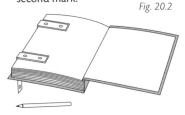

Fig. 20.2

③ With the bracket tracings made in step 2 as your guide, use the craft knife to cut partway into the inside back cover (cut deep enough, about ½", so that when the bracket is in place, the book cover closes easily) (fig. 20.3).

Fig. 20.3

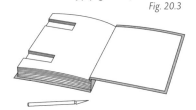

④ Insert the two L-brackets into the cutaways. Make marks where the brackets cross the front cover. Use the craft knife to cut two small notches into the cover at those marks so that the brackets can hang flush after they're inserted into the book.

⑤ Drill the brackets into the book (fig. 20.5).

Fig. 20.5

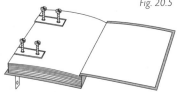

⑥ Close the back cover and drill a screw into the center of the back cover to keep the book closed.

⑦ Flip the book over and drill the other side of the L-brackets to the wall (fig. 20.7). Then pile on the books.

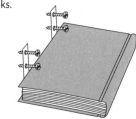

Fig. 20.7

Secret Stash Beaded Curtain

LEVEL ⊗ ⊗ ⊗ ○ ○

When you start putting in requests to friends and family for empty toilet paper rolls, you'll likely get a lot of quizzical looks and skepticism. But when you install this simple, geometric, modern beaded curtain, those skeptics will be changing their tune! Another humble material rescued from the recycling bin.

WHAT YOU NEED

- String
- Scissors
- Tape measure
- 12 to 15 empty toilet paper rolls or 4 to 5 paper towel rolls
- 3 colors of craft paint (sample uses pink, yellow, and orange)
- Large sharp sewing needle
- Tension rod, sized to fit your doorway
- Hot glue gun and glue
- Small foam brush

1. To determine the number and length of pieces of string to use, measure the height and width of the doorway where you plan to hang the divider. Divide the width measurement by two to determine the number of pieces of string you'll need (the strings will hang 2" apart), and cut the pieces to the length of the doorway plus 1'. (*Example:* This doorway is 8' high and 30" wide, so 15 lengths of 9' string were cut.) Set aside the rest of the string for use in step 8.

2. Flatten one of the toilet paper rolls slightly and cut through it every ¼" to make paper rings (fig. 21.2). Repeat with the rest of the rolls to make approximately eighteen rings. (A paper towel roll will yield about forty-four rings.) The rings will be a little flattened already and that's the ideal shape to work with.

3. Separate out seventy-two rings to paint, then split them into three equal piles of twenty-four rings each. Use the foam brush to carefully paint a different color on the outside of the rings in each pile. Let dry.

4. Select one of the pieces of string you cut in step 1 and double knot it at one end. Thread the opposite end onto the needle.

5. Poke the needle through one point of one of the toilet paper rings. Make a knot in the string about 2" above the end knot. Then poke the needle through the second point of the ring (fig. 21.5).

6. Continue to string the rings, making a double knot at the

Fig. 21.2

bottom where you want your ring to sit and a single knot above the ring to secure it (fig. 21.6). You can add on rings at random (as shown) or add them every few inches or so.

Fig. 21.5–6

7 Repeat steps 4 through 6 with the remaining pieces of string.

8 Install the tension rod about 6" down from the top of the door frame and adjust it to fit tightly. Apply a dot of hot glue at one end of the rod and start wrapping the string around tightly, taking care not to show any of the rod. Continue until the rod is completely wrapped and glue at the end to finish.

9 Tie each string onto the tension rod about 2" apart, with an overhand knot, and trim any excess string with scissors (fig. 21.9).

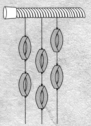

Fig. 21.9

Totally Tubular

The first documented use of toilet paper in human history dates back to the sixth century A.D. in early medieval China. For Emperor Hongwu's imperial family alone, 15,000 sheets of special toilet paper were made, with each sheet of paper perfumed. Though people had been using toilet paper for centuries, no one thought of putting it on a paper tube roll until Zeth Wheeler got the patent in 1877.

22 | Globetrotter Photo Mat

LEVEL ⊗ ⊗ ⊗ ⊗ ⊗

You posted those photos of the trip to the Grand Canyon and the last family reunion at the lake on Facebook, but why not get them off the Internet and allow them to grace your real walls? Better yet, let the map you used on that road trip find new life sprucing up an inexpensive frame. Try a whole bunch of them hung on your walls gallery-style for almost instant wall decor!

WHAT YOU NEED

- A frame with a precut mat
- Ruler
- Pencil
- Craft knife
- Self-healing cutting mat
- Road map (at least 2" wider and longer than the mat)
- Foam brush
- White glue

1. Remove the mat from the frame and measure the outer dimensions (x" × y"). Add 2" to both the height and width (x + 2", y + 2").

2. Use the ruler, pencil, craft knife, and cutting mat to cut an (x + 2") × (y + 2") rectangle from the road map.

3. Brush glue over the front of the photo mat and press it, centered, onto the road map piece.

4. Measure, mark, and cut a rectangle from the center of the road map that is 1" smaller than the window of the photo mat. Then cut a 45-degree diagonal slit into the road map at each inner corner (fig. 22.4).

5. Use the craft knife to miter each corner of the road map at a 45-degree angle (fig. 22.5). Remove the triangles of paper.

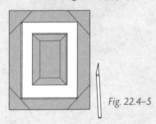

Fig. 22.4–5

6. Brush glue along the inner and outer road map edges and fold and press the edges over to the back of the photo mat (fig. 22.6). Let dry before reassembling the frame.

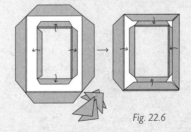

Fig. 22.6

23 | Photo Cube

My husband took a handful of beautiful photos of his bike commute on his Holga camera, and I thought they deserved a little attention—the desk drawer where they were stuffed was rather unbecoming. I made this project for him. Photo cubes are a cool way to display your photos outside of an album (or a drawer). Depending on how you decorate it, the photo cube would also make a great farewell gift for a friend who's moving or a special way to announce a wedding or new baby.

WHAT YOU NEED

- Access to a computer with a printer
- 6 digital photos
- 6 sheets of photo paper 4" × 6"
- Ruler
- Craft knife
- Self-healing cutting mat
- Cardboard packaging
- Foam brush
- White glue
- Hot glue gun and glue
- Bag of dried beans (optional)

1. Using the photo program of your choice, crop each of the six photos into a 4" × 4" square.

2. Print each photo on 4" × 6" photo paper, setting your preferences so that the photos will print in the center of the photo paper.

3. Use the ruler, craft knife, and cutting mat to diagonally cut the corners of the extra inch of paper that is on either side of each photo (fig. 23.3). (This will leave a trapezoid-shaped paper flap on two sides of each photo.)

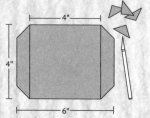

Fig. 23.3

4. Cut six 4" × 6" pieces of cardboard (fig. 23.4). One at a time, brush glue onto the back of each photo and press it to a piece of cardboard. Let dry, then trim off the excess cardboard corners.

Fig. 23.4

5. Working on the wrong side of each piece, use a craft knife and ruler to carefully score along each flap.

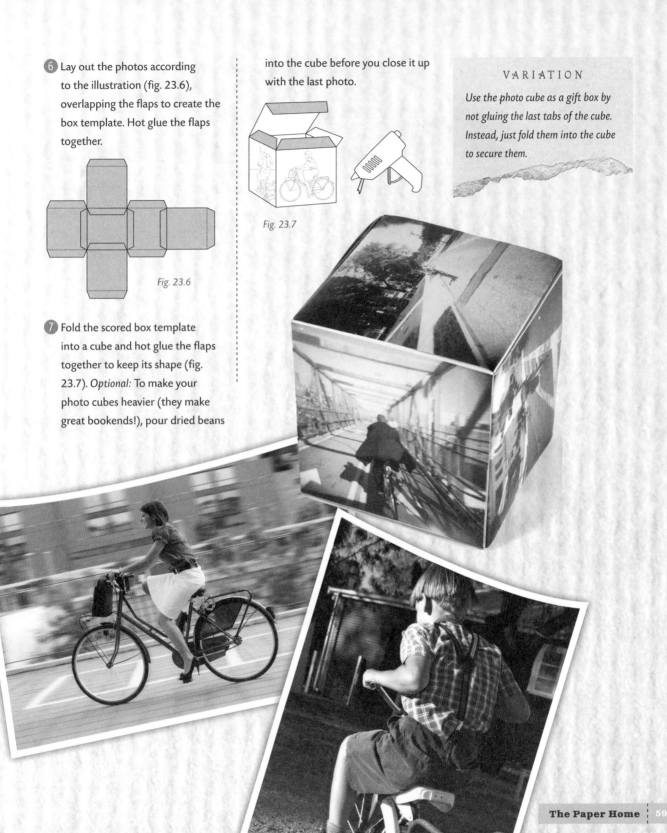

6 Lay out the photos according to the illustration (fig. 23.6), overlapping the flaps to create the box template. Hot glue the flaps together.

Fig. 23.6

7 Fold the scored box template into a cube and hot glue the flaps together to keep its shape (fig. 23.7). *Optional:* To make your photo cubes heavier (they make great bookends!), pour dried beans

into the cube before you close it up with the last photo.

Fig. 23.7

VARIATION

Use the photo cube as a gift box by not gluing the last tabs of the cube. Instead, just fold them into the cube to secure them.

24

Kirigami Wallflowers

LEVEL ❌❌❌ⓧⓧ

Too old for those Monet posters from museum shops, but too broke for fine art? It's time to think of art outside the frame. A cluster of one-of-a-kind kirigami (a variation of origami) flowers is a rich bouquet for your blank walls, all year long. Bonus: They are easy to hang, just as easy to take down, and absolutely addictive to make—oh, and they won't wilt.

WHAT YOU NEED

- *Ruler*
- *Craft knife*
- *Self-healing cutting mat*
- *Tissue paper in 3 to 5 colors*
- *Scissors*
- *Pencil*
- *Book or other heavy, flat object*
- *Double-sided tape*

1. Use the ruler, craft knife, and cutting mat to cut tissue paper squares that measure from 3" to 1'. *Note:* Each square represents one flower.

2. Lay flat one square of tissue paper. Fold the paper in half diagonally, corner to corner, to form a triangle (fig. 24.2).

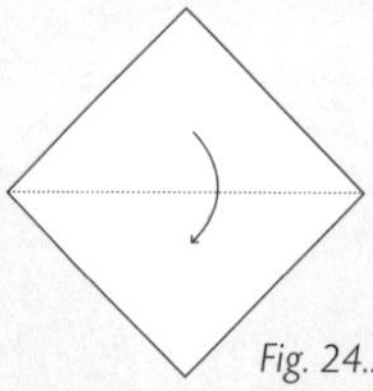

Fig. 24.2

3. Fold the triangle in half to form a smaller triangle, and unfold (fig. 24.3)

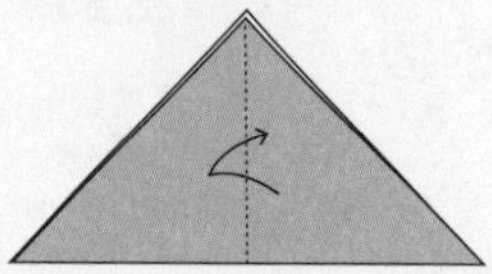

Fig. 24.3

4. Fold one point in toward the center at a 60-degree angle, as shown. Fold over the other point the remaining 30 degrees so that its edge lines up with the other side (fig. 24.4).

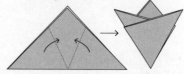

Fig. 24.4

5. Fold the paper piece in half and crease (fig. 24.5).

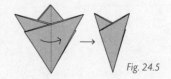

Fig. 24.5

6. Snip off the top points (fig. 24.6).

Fig. 24.6

7 With a pencil, draw a design on the front of the folded tissue paper (fig. 24.7). *Optional:* Use the illustrations as inspiration, but freestyling is encouraged!

Fig. 24.7

8 Use the craft knife to cut out the traced shapes (fig. 24.8), making sure you cut through all of the folded layers.

Fig. 24.8

9 Very carefully unfold the paper to reveal a kirigami flower.

10 Repeat steps 2 through 9 on the remaining paper squares.

11 Place the flowers in a book for a few days to flatten.

12 To hang each flower, attach a single piece of double-sided tape at the top of the flower.

VARIATION

• If your kirigami flower's no wallflower, hang it from the window or the ceiling. Glue flowers to cards or gift bags, mat them on contrasting paper and frame them, or decoupage them to a tray or small piece of furniture.

• Out of tissue paper? Try using newspaper, magazines, or origami paper to make kirigami flowers.

• When the weather turns cold, use white printer paper to make traditional cut-paper snowflakes.

25

Into the Woods
Scherenschnitte

LEVEL ⊗ ⊗ ⊗ ⊗ ⊗

WHAT YOU NEED

. . . .

- *Access to a computer with a printer*

- Scherenschnitte *templates**

- *Tracing paper*

- *Pencil*

- *A piece (8"× 8") of black, dark brown, and light brown paper*

- *Small scraps of white and green paper (2" or larger squares)*

- *Craft knife*

- *Self-healing cutting mat*

- *Glue stick*

*S*cherenschnitte, meaning "scissor cuts" in German, is an art tradition dating all the way back to the 1500s. This paper art features painstakingly fine cuts that create incredibly detailed designs. Though time-consuming, *Scherenschnitte* is actually pretty easy when you break it down: Just take a deep breath and start cutting piece by piece. When you're done, mat your work on a contrasting color, frame it, and admire your incredible handiwork. This particular *Scherenschnitte* design is inspired by magical woodland scenes, but once you know the technique, creating your own scenes is a snip . . . err, *snap!*

1 Print the *Scherenschnitte* templates onto printer paper. Use the pencil to transfer the designs onto tracing paper, then trace over the pencil lines to transfer the design onto the colored paper. Trace template 1 onto the sheet of dark brown paper, template 2 onto light brown paper, template detail 1 onto the white scraps, and template detail 2 onto the green scraps (fig. 25.1).

Fig. 25.1

* Download at workman.com/papermade

2 Use the craft knife and cutting mat to cut out the shapes (figs. 25.2a, 25.2b, and 25.2c).

Fig. 25.2a

Fig. 25.2b

Fig. 25.2c

3 Coat the back of the dark brown cutout with a glue stick and center it on the black paper (fig. 25.3). Repeat for the light brown cutout, layering it over the dark brown cutout.

Fig. 25.3

4 Add glue to the backs of the white and the green details and stick them in place over the light brown cutout (fig. 25.4). Let dry.

Fig. 25.4

5 Trim the paper as needed.

WHAT YOU NEED

- *Scraps of wallpaper*
- *Small scissors*
- *Wallpaper paste*
- *Paintbrush*
- *Brayer*
- *Sponge*

26 Not So Straight and Narrow Wallpaper Border

LEVEL ✪✪✪○○

A couple of years ago I covered one wall in my kitchen with some amazing wallpaper. A year later, I did the same thing in my living room. After both projects were done, I was left with a bunch of little pieces and the classic Goldilocks situation: The scraps were too big to throw away but too small to complete another wall. They're perfect, however, for making this oh-so-whimsical wallpaper border. Be sure to look for wallpapers that have distinct, easy-to-cut motifs. And don't feel limited to flowers—a flock of birds or a grove of wallpaper trees sprouting from your baseboards would be stunning, too!

❶ Unroll the wallpaper pieces, right side up. Determine the shapes and designs you'd like to use from the pattern. Then use scissors to cut them out (fig. 26.1).

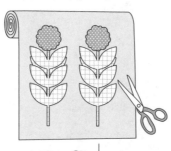

Fig. 26.1

❷ Brush the back of the wallpaper motif with wallpaper paste and press it to the wall. (The sample shown here begins at the top edge of the baseboard.) Use the brayer to smooth out any bubbles (fig. 26.2).

Fig. 26.2

3 Continue working each piece from the bottom of the motif to the top, brushing a section with paste, pressing it carefully to the wall, and then using the brayer to smooth out bubbles.

4 When you're done, use the sponge to wipe excess wallpaper paste from the wall (fig. 26.4).

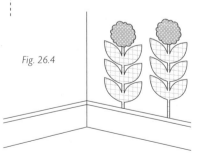

Fig. 26.4

VARIATION

• *Try other paper sources! Line a room with vintage sheet music. Seek out children's lullabies for a traditional nursery, or old standards in a living room—or change it up with rock 'n' roll for your little one and operettas for the bathroom! Sheet music comes in two standard sizes: 10" × 13" and 9" × 12", so it's easy to estimate how much you will need for your project.*

• *Use any kind of book pages for a border. How about pages from an old dictionary to complete a library? So cute! Or if you really want to go the distance, cover the whole wall with book pages!*

WHAT YOU NEED

- *Access to a computer with a printer and paper*
- *Chandelier templates**
- *Craft knife*
- *Self-healing cutting mat*
- *Large cardboard box (approximately 3' × 2')*
- *Painter's tape*
- *Pencil*
- *Foam brush*
- *Acrylic paint in desired shade*
- *Floral wire*
- *Wire cutters*
- *Awl*
- *Hammer*
- *Hanging lantern cord kit*
- *LED lightbulb*

27 | Modern Fête Silhouette Chandelier

LEVEL ✖ ✖ ✖ ✖

Who needs antique Murano glass? This lamp takes the very essence of the chandelier—its intricate and delicate shape—and turns fussy and old-fashioned into supermodern and graphic. This project takes a lot of careful cutting but practically no money to make, so it's a good rainy weekend project. Use an LED lightbulb to light it up—it's a greener choice (they use a lot less energy than standard bulbs) and it gives off less heat (which is the better option when you're pairing a bulb with a paper structure!).

1. Print the chandelier templates (1a, 1b, 1c, and 2a, 2b, and 2c). Use the craft knife and cutting mat to cut them out.

2. Flatten the cardboard box and arrange template pages 1a, 1b, and 1c on one side. Tape them in place and use a pencil to trace around them (fig. 27.2).

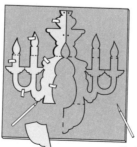

Fig. 27.2

3. Peel up the templates, flip them, and arrange them to mirror the tracing you made in step 2. Tape them in place and trace around them.

4. Cut out the entire silhouette.

5. Repeat steps 2–4 with template 2 to create the second piece.

6. Paint both sides and edges of the cardboard silhouettes with the foam brush (fig. 27.6). Let dry and paint one more coat.

Fig. 27.6

* Download at workman.com/papermade

7 Cut two 5" pieces of floral wire with wire cutters. Give them two coats of paint, letting them dry fully between coats.

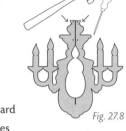

8 Use the awl and hammer to punch holes, as marked on the templates, into the two cardboard chandelier silhouettes (fig. 27.8).

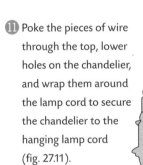

Fig. 27.8

9 Slide the two pieces together where the slits are cut, aligning the pieces perpendicularly (fig. 27.9).

10 Follow the manufacturer's instructions to assemble the lantern cord kit. Then hang it at the desired height.

Fig. 27.9

11 Poke the pieces of wire through the top, lower holes on the chandelier, and wrap them around the lamp cord to secure the chandelier to the hanging lamp cord (fig. 27.11).

Fig. 27.11

12 Adjust the lamp assembly so the bulb is hanging in the open space of the chandelier before turning it on.

(makes 2 frames)

- *Access to a computer with a printer and paper*
- *Small and large frame templates**
- *Pencil*
- *Scissors*
- *1 large or 2 medium-size (about 18" × 12" × 12") cardboard boxes*
- *Craft knife*
- *Self-healing cutting mat*
- *White glue*
- *2 sawtooth metal hangers with nails*
- *Small hammer*

28 | Broke for Baroque Frames

LEVEL ⊗⊗⊗⊗⊗

everal years ago I was looking through a home design book and saw a series of incredibly ornate frames hung over an equally impressive mantel. They were in the home of a French designer, and I imagined that they were antiques passed down from a distant relative with an obscure royal lineage. But when I looked closer, I realized they were made of cardboard! These cardboard frames, fit for a king or queen, are an homage to that idea.

❶ Print the small and large frame templates and cut them out using scissors. Since each template is one quarter of the frame, trace the top quarter with a pencil on the cardboard, flip the template, lining it up carefully with your pencil marks, and trace the other side (fig. 28.1). Repeat with the bottom quarter to complete the frame. The large frame is symmetrical, so the same template will be traced four times.

❷ Use the craft knife and cutting mat to cut out your frames.

❸ Use the craft knife to cut 1½"–2" leaves and thin strips from the cardboard and add them symmetrically to decorate the frames. To make the swirls, cut ⅛"-wide cardboard strips and coil the ends in opposite directions. Glue on each piece with white glue (fig. 28.3).

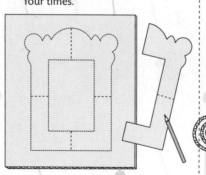

Fig. 28.1

Fig. 28.3

* Download at workman.com/papermade

4 Let dry. To prepare the frames for hanging, center a sawtooth hook about 2" down from the top back of each frame, dip the sharp end of each nail into glue, and gently hammer them in. Then hang from a nail or screw in the wall.

Wallpaper Collaged Side Table

29

LEVEL ✪ ✪ ✪ ✪ ✪

Vintage wallpaper is one of my favorite mediums to work with. The colors and the patterns are breathtaking, and though entire rolls of vintage wallpaper are very pricey, it's easy to find small scraps packaged together at thrift stores and flea markets for next to nothing. If you can't find vintage wallpaper, ask your friends and family if they have any wallpaper scraps left over from decorating projects, or collect bits of unused wrapping paper. The fun in this table is the randomness of the collage, so be free!

WHAT YOU NEED

- Small wood or particle board side table (for example, the Lack table from IKEA)
- Pinking shears
- Wallpaper scraps in different patterns and colors
- Foam brush
- Decoupage medium
- Brayer

1 If the legs of the table unscrew, remove the legs and set them aside.

2 Use the pinking shears to cut about twenty different-size squares and rectangles from the wallpaper scraps. (My largest piece covered the entire top of the table, while the smallest was a 2" square.) Arrange them on top of the table (fig. 29.2).

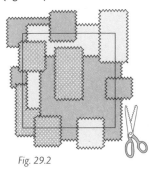

Fig. 29.2

3 Beginning with the larger pieces, one at a time brush the back of the wallpaper with the decoupage medium and press onto the tabletop. Use the brayer to smooth any wrinkles in the wallpaper.

4 Cover the rest of the top and sides of the tabletop with the smaller pieces of wallpaper (fig. 29.4).

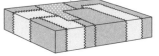

Fig. 29.4

5 Repeat steps 3 and 4 for the legs of the table. Cover one entire table leg with a large piece of wallpaper, taking care to keep the wallpaper

smooth and even at the corners of the legs. Then add smaller pieces of contrasting paper over it (fig. 29.5).

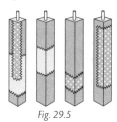

Fig. 29.5

6 Let the table pieces dry, and reattach the table legs if they were removed in step 1. To finish, brush on one coat of decoupage medium to cover the entire table, and then let it dry completely. Brush on one last coat and let dry.

30

Butterfly Box

LEVEL ⊗ ⊗ ⊗ ⊗ ⊗

WHAT YOU NEED

- *Access to a computer with a printer and paper*
- *Butterfly templates**
- *Craft knife*
- *Self-healing cutting mat*
- *Small flat gift box (a scarf box is perfect)*
- *Ruler*
- *Pencil*
- *Foam brush*
- *White glue*
- *4 to 6 book pages (for 1 box)*
- *Wallpaper scraps*
- *Map pins*
- *Small (approximately ¾" × 2½") scraps of white paper*
- *Typewriter (optional)*
- *Clear vellum (optional)*

This is a cruelty-free butterfly collection; all the beauty of delicate wings can adorn your walls without harming a single fluttering insect! The vintage wallpaper scraps are a nod to the rich history of the hobby of butterfly collecting. Group a few of these boxes together on a wall or a shelf for the most impact.

1 Print the butterfly templates and cut them out using the craft knife and the cutting mat. Set them aside.

2 Open the box and lay the lid right side down on the cutting mat. Use the ruler and pencil to measure and mark 2" in from all four sides of the lid. Connect the marks to form a rectangle (fig. 30.2).

3 Cut out the rectangle, and set it aside (fig. 30.3).

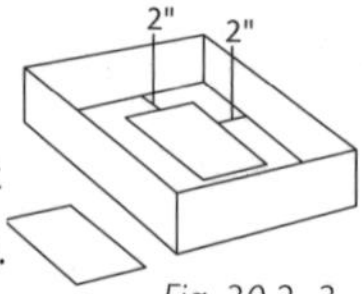

Fig. 30.2–3

4 Brush glue generously over the outside of the lid (fig. 30.4). One at a time, press the book pages flat into the glue to cover the lid. Repeat to cover the rectangle that was cut out in step 3.

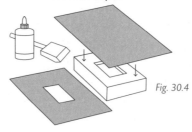

Fig. 30.4

5 Fold the outside edges of the paper pages to the inside of the lid and secure them with glue. Likewise, fold over the edges of paper around the rectangle piece (fig. 30.5). *Note:* The inside of the lid and the back of the rectangle won't be visible when the project is done.

Fig. 30.5

6 Lay the lid right side down again and cut an X into the paper page that covers the window of the box lid. Brush with glue and fold the paper triangles back to stick to the inside of the lid (fig. 30.6).

Fig. 30.6

* Download at workman.com/papermade

7 Repeat steps 4 and 5 to cover the inside of the box (fig. 30.7). *Note: The outside of the box won't be visible when the project is done.*

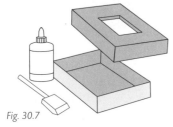

Fig. 30.7

8 Use the pencil to trace two to four butterflies (depending on the size of the box) onto the blank side of the wallpaper scraps. Cut them out with the craft knife (fig. 30.8).

Fig. 30.8

9 Gently fold the wings back at both sides of the body to make them more dimensional (fig. 30.9).

Fig. 30.9

10 Brush a small amount of glue on the underside of the butterfly bodies (avoid the wings), and press them into the inside of the box as desired. Push a map pin into the body of each butterfly (fig. 30.10).

Fig. 30.10

11 Research the names of various butterflies and handwrite or type their scientific names on scraps of white paper. Cut the scraps into ¾" × 2½" rectangles and glue them into the box as butterfly identification labels (fig. 30.11).

Fig. 30.11

12 Place the lid onto the box to complete the frame and ready it for display. *Optional:* Cut a piece of protective clear vellum to fit into the inside lid of the box and glue it into place around the inside edge.

31 | Tord's Lamp

LEVEL ⊗ ⊗ ⊗ ⊗ ⊗

WHAT YOU NEED

- *Access to a computer with a printer and paper*
- *Vine templates**
- *Craft knife*
- *Self-healing cutting mat*
- *Scissors*
- *12 to 15 waterproof 9" × 12" envelopes (such as Tyvek envelopes; tell your friends and family you are collecting them!)*
- *Pencil*
- *Small lamp ring with a top for a pendant light*
- *White glue*
- *Binder clips*

This lamp is heavily influenced by one of my favorite designers, Tord Boontje. Since imitation is the sincerest form of flattery and money doesn't grow on trees, I decided to reimagine a Tord Boontje lamp, DIY-style. *A note on paper lamps and safety:* Tyvek is flame-retardant, so it is a great material for the paper vines. The lantern base adds another layer of safety. Still, it is best to unplug and turn off all lamps when you aren't home.

— ◆ —

1. Print the vine templates and cut them out using a craft knife and the cutting mat.

2. Use scissors to cut open the envelopes on two sides (plus the opening) so that you can lay them flat (fig. 31.2).

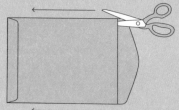

Fig. 31.2

3. Trace the vine templates onto the envelopes and use the craft knife and cutting mat to cut them out (fig. 31.3). The vine templates are just a guideline—move them around on the Tyvek to make the vines longer or shorter. Cut enough

vines to line the lamp ring. (The sample used about fifty vines of different lengths to cover a lamp ring 7" in diameter.)

Fig. 31.3

4. Squeeze a 2" line of glue at the end of one of the vines, wrap it around the ring, and glue it to itself (fig. 31.4).

Fig. 31.4

* Download at workman.com/papermade

5 Repeat step 4 with two more vines, and then pinch a binder clip over the tops of the vines to hold them while the glue dries (fig. 31.5).

Fig. 31.5

6 Continue adding vines until you have covered the lamp ring. Let dry and remove the binder clips.

❖

Fractal Rock

While many paper artists are inspired by the blank page, artist Jen Stark's (www.jenstark .com) paper sculptures literally burst off of the page in shocks of color. Inspired by anatomical textbooks, wormholes, and fractals, Stark's work only looks wild and chaotic. In fact, each paper cut is incredibly exact.

WHAT YOU NEED

• Access to a computer with a printer and paper

• Pencil

• Flower templates*

• Tracing paper

• 11" × 30" piece of brown craft paper

• Craft knife

• Self-healing cutting mat

• Small foam brush

• White glue

• 11" × 30" piece of contrasting colored paper

• 2 wire lamp rings (8"), 1 with a clip top

• Binder clips

32 **Paper Cuts Lamp Shade**

LEVEL ✪ ✪ ✪ ✪

T his may look like a plain-Jane craft paper shade, but all you have to do is flip the light switch to see how plain this shade *isn't*. A bouquet of delicate cut paper flowers reveals a bright glowing turquoise paper beneath. Turquoise is my favorite color, but you should feel free to choose any shade for your new shade.

1 Print the flower templates. Use a pencil to trace the shapes onto a sheet of tracing paper (fig. 32.1).

Fig. 32.1

2 Lay the piece of brown craft paper flat and determine where to place the flowers.

3 Flip the flower tracing (so the pencil side is down) and carefully trace over the flower, transferring the design to the paper.

4 Lift the flower tracing and place it again to make a second tracing. Continue transferring flowers this way, pausing as needed to retrace the design from the template.

5 Use the craft knife and cutting mat to cut along the lines of the flower designs. Be sure you cut only the lines and not all the way through or you will end up cutting out the entire flower (fig. 32.5).

Fig. 32.5

6 When you have finished cutting each flower, flip the paper over. Brush some glue over the paper, avoiding the flower designs. Quickly and carefully press it to the colored paper, making sure to line up the edges, to create the shade (fig. 32.6).

Fig. 32.6

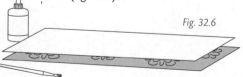

* Download at workman.com/papermade

7 Carefully wrap the shade around the clip top and use clips to attach it to the ring at the top. Use a pencil to mark the spot where the edges overlap (fig. 32.7).

Fig. 32.7

8 Remove the shade and brush a line of glue along the mark you made in step 7. Gently roll the paper so the edges line up to create a tube. Lay the glue bottle (closed, of course) or an item of similar weight over the seam while it dries (fig. 32.8). Let dry about 30 minutes.

Fig. 32.8

9 Brush a line of glue along the inside edge of the top of the tube. Fit the clip top into the tube and secure it in place with the clips (fig. 32.9). Let dry about 30 minutes.

Fig. 32.9

33 (Not Exactly a) Full Deck Lamp Shade

LEVEL ✖ ✖ ✖ ⊗ ⊗

Card games have always been a major pastime in my family. My grandmother kept a carved wooden box of playing cards on the windowsill in the dining room so that afternoon card games could start immediately after lunch. While a full deck of cards can provide hours of entertainment, a not-so-full deck is, to most, trash. Put those cards to good use and transform them into a lamp shade instead!

WHAT YOU NEED

- 22 playing cards
- Painter's tape
- Access to a sewing machine, and thread in desired color
- Scissors
- ⅛" circle hole punch
- 2 wire lamp shade rings (8"), 1 with a clip top
- Flat-nose pliers
- 22 jump rings

1. Lay down two rows of eleven faceup playing cards in any order.

2. Working from left to right on the first row, take the first and the second card and line them up right next to each other so that the edges meet but don't overlap. Secure them temporarily with a little piece of painter's tape (fig. 33.2).

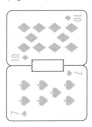

Fig. 33.2

3. Set the sewing machine to a zigzag stitch, and backstitching at the beginning and end to secure them, sew the two cards together, removing the tape before you reach it (fig. 33.3). Clip the threads with the scissors.

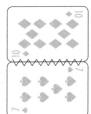

Fig. 33.3

4. Repeat steps 2 and 3 to add the third card to the second, the fourth to the third, and so on.

Practical Magic

Decks of cards are said to have had religious, mystical, or astrological significance. Each suit of 13 cards represents the 13 months of the lunar year. Similarly, the whole deck of the 52 cards represents the 52 weeks of the year.

5 Continue sewing the cards together in the first row. Then stitch together the cards in the second row (fig. 33.5). You should have two stitched rows of 11 cards each.

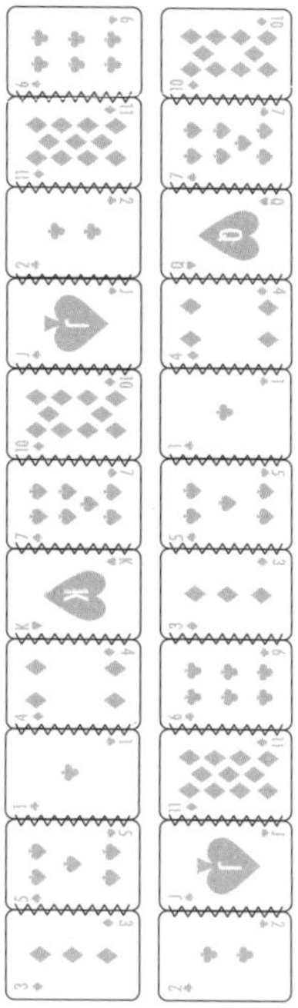

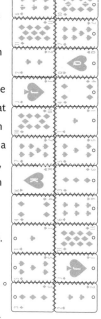

Fig. 33.5

6 Line up the first and second rows so that the edges of the cards just meet. Tape them in place. Then sew the two rows together with a zigzag stitch, backstitching at the beginning and end to secure them, removing the tape before you reach it. Clip the threads with scissors.

7 With a hole punch, make a centered hole about ¼" from the edge of each card in the top row. Repeat for the bottom row, punching a hole, centered, about ¼" from the bottom edge of each card (fig. 33.7).

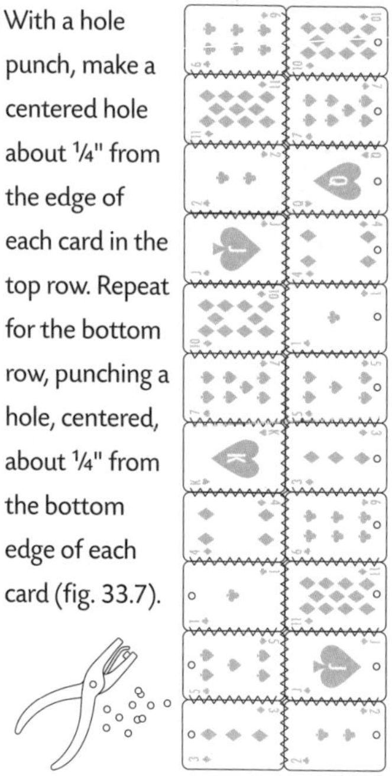

Fig. 33.7

8 To begin attaching the cards to the clip-top ring, use the pliers to open up a jump ring (fig. 33.8).

Fig. 33.8

9 Guide the jump ring through one of the punched holes of the cards and then over the lamp-shade ring. Be sure that the clip of the ring is facing down. Then use the pliers to tightly close the jump ring (fig. 33.9).

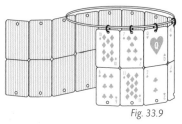

Fig. 33.9

10 Repeat steps 8 and 9 until the top row of cards is completely connected to the lamp-shade ring. The ends of the two rows of cards will overlap slightly, making the structure more stable.

11 Repeat steps 8 and 9 for the bottom lamp ring (fig. 33.11).

Fig. 33.11

By the Numbers Keepsake Box

34

LEVEL ⊗ ⊗ ⊗ ⊗ ⊗

WHAT YOU NEED
. . . .

- Ruler
- Craft knife
- Self-healing cutting mat
- Paint-by-number painting (at least 11" × 17")
- Small foam brush
- White glue
- Sheet of colored paper, at least 6 ½" wide and 17" long (for the lining)
- Pencil
- Wood glue
- 2 small C-clamps
- 6" leather cord

Paint-by-number kits were first introduced in the 1950s when the United States economy was booming. Americans had an unprecedented amount of leisure time and were taking up new hobbies like nobody's business. Today, it's pretty easy to find finished paint-by-number works, and since they were made by hobbyists and not skilled artists, they are usually pretty cheap. I collect paint-by-number work and would never advocate the cutting up of a really good one, but sometimes the years take their toll on these paintings and leave them ripped and torn. These are perfect for upcycling into little boxes for stowing away any treasured possessions.

1 With the ruler, craft knife, and cutting mat, cut a 2" × 17" and 4½" × 11" rectangle from the painting.

2 Brush the back of both pieces of the painting with white glue and press them to the colored paper. Trim the excess colored paper with a craft knife.

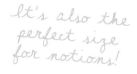

It's also the perfect size for notions!

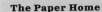

3 Lay the 2" × 17" piece (A) lengthwise, painted side up. Measure and lightly mark three lines 4¼" apart. Score along the lines with the craft knife and gently bend (fig. 34.3). Set aside.

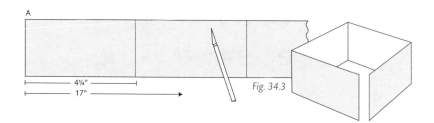

Fig. 34.3

4 Lay the 4½" × 11" piece (B) lengthwise, painted side up. Measure and lightly mark a line 4½" in from each edge. Score along the lines with a craft knife and gently bend as shown (fig. 34.4).

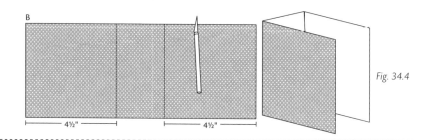

Fig. 34.4

5 Fold piece A into a square, and brush a line of wood glue along the open 2" edges. Clamp together with a C-clamp to dry (fig. 34.5). This is the interior of the box.

Fig. 34.5

6 Brush the bottom edges of the square with wood glue. Line up one edge of the box with the inner scored edge of one of the square panels of piece B to create the bottom of the box. Clamp in place to dry (fig. 34.6).

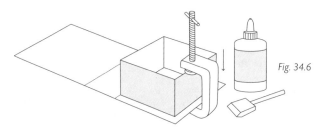

Fig. 34.6

7 Brush the inside of the small panel on piece B with glue and attach it to the side of the box. Clamp in place to dry (fig. 34.7).

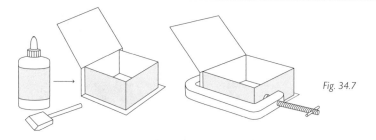

Fig. 34.7

8 To make the top closure, cut a ½" × 1" rectangle and a ½" square from the painting. Center and glue the ½" square onto the back of the rectangle. Then center and glue the square along the top of the box, ½" away from the front edge (fig. 34.8).

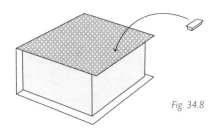

Fig. 34.8

9 Repeat step 8 to make the front closure, centering it along the front panel, ½" from the top edge (fig. 34.9). Let dry.

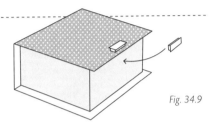

Fig. 34.9

10 To latch the box, tie one end of the leather cord around the front closure and wrap it around the top closure from left to right, then down around the bottom from right to left, forming a figure 8 (fig. 34.10).

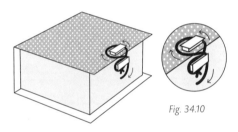

Fig. 34.10

35

This Heart Is an Open Box

LEVEL ✪ ✪ ✪ ○ ○

Books with hidden compartments strike the perfect balance of mystery and romance, as in old spy movies, where concealed buttons in dusty old libraries reveal secret passageways. They're a perfect place for stashing something very close to your heart: old love notes, a cameo, photos from your first wedding in Vegas that you never told anyone about (just kidding!). But speaking of weddings, this hidden book could be a really good setup for a proposal! You heard it here first.

WHAT YOU NEED

- *Access to a computer with a printer and paper*
- *Heart template**
- *Scissors*
- *Hardcover book that's past its prime*
- *Foam brush*
- *White glue*
- *Extra books or other weights*
- *Pencil*
- *Craft knife*

1. Print the heart template and cut it out using scissors.

2. Open the book at the front cover and brush glue over the edges of the pages along all three unbound sides (fig. 35.2).

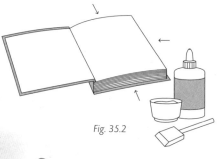

Fig. 35.2

3. Leaving the front cover open, stack a few books (or something of similar weight) on top of the pages of the book, and let it dry overnight.

4. Center and trace the heart template onto the first page of the book (fig. 35.4).

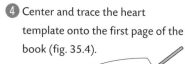

Fig. 35.4

5. Use the craft knife to carefully cut the traced heart shape into the book. Cut just a few layers at a time, remove the cut pieces, and repeat. Cut straight down into the book to make sure the heart shape is even (fig. 35.5).

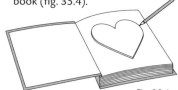

Fig. 35.5

* Download at workman.com/papermade

6 Repeat step 5 until the heart has reached the desired depth. Then brush the inside edges of the heart with glue, stack a few books on top of the pages, and let dry completely (fig. 35.6).

Fig. 35.6

36 Dogwood Paper Blossoms

LEVEL ✪ ✪ ✪ ✪ ✪

Double-sided crepe paper mimics the delicate flowers of dogwood branches. This flower arrangement will look as good ten years from now as it does the day you "grow" it. If you don't have a backyard, make a stop at your local park to scout for small fallen tree branches. You may get some odd looks, but you will definitely find plenty of good branches for this project—and be tidying up the neighborhood in the meantime!

1 Print and cut out the flower and bud templates.

2 Count the tips of your branches to determine how many flowers and buds you need for your arrangement. Trace the flower and bud templates onto the crepe paper as many times as needed and cut them out. Erase any stray pencil marks.

3 To give the flowers dimension, gently fold each petal of the flowers in half lengthwise toward the front of the flower (fig. 36.3a). Fold the buds in half widthwise (fig. 36.3b).

Fig. 36.3a

Fig. 36.3b

4 To make the flower centers, tear a tiny piece of ½" white tissue paper and roll into a ball. Make three balls per flower and hot glue them to the center of each flower (fig. 36.4).

Fig. 36.4

5 One at a time, squeeze hot glue onto the tips of the branches and press on the flowers. To attach the buds, fold them around the tips of the branches (fig. 36.5).

Fig. 36.5

6 Arrange your everlasting bouquet!

WHAT YOU NEED

- Access to a computer with a printer and paper
- Flower and bud templates*
- Scissors
- 8 to 12 branches (or enough to fill a vase)
- Pencil
- Scraps of double-sided crepe paper
- Small scrap of white tissue paper
- Hot glue gun and glue

* Download at workman.com/papermade

- Ruler

- Pencil

- 20 large (approximately 18"× 18"× 24") corrugated cardboard boxes

- Utility knife

- Self-healing cutting mat

- Wood glue

- Foam brush

- C-clamps

37 Never Bored Cardboard Table

LEVEL ✪ ✪ ✪ ✪ ✪

Cardboard is a very useful material, used primarily for packaging (think moving, delivery, storage). As you've learned in the pages of this book, it can be made into fancy frames, small shelves, or shaped into 3-D papier-mâché wall decor. But here is the ultimate test of the utility of cardboard: furniture! This project takes a little bit of time and a whole lotta cutting, but it is a showstopper. Every time someone asks you where you got your cool cardboard table and you get to answer, "Oh, that? I made it," it will be totally worth it.

❶ Use the ruler and pencil to draw a 14½" × 17" squared-off U-shape on the side of a flattened cardboard box, oriented on the cardboard so that the U runs perpendicular to the corrugation. Then draw a 3½" × 19" rectangle, oriented so the long edge of the rectangle runs perpendicular to the corrugation (fig. 37.1).

❷ Use the ruler, utility knife, and cutting mat to cut out the shapes (fig. 37.2).

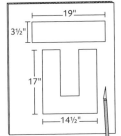

Fig. 37.1–2

❸ Trace and cut the U-shape forty-five times from the remaining cardboard box pieces to create a total of forty-six table pieces (for the table legs). Trace and cut the rectangle eighty-four times to create a total of eighty-five pieces (for the tabletop).

❹ Squeeze wood glue onto one side of the table leg pieces. Align and press it against another leg piece (fig. 37.4). Let dry.

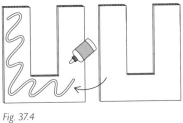

Fig. 37.4

❺ Glue and place a third piece against the two pieces glued in step 4. Repeat with all remaining table leg pieces (fig. 37.5).

Fig. 37.5

❻ Repeat steps 4 and 5 with the tabletop pieces (fig. 37.6).

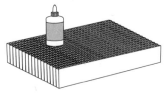

Fig. 37.6

❼ Clamp the two stacks of table pieces and let dry overnight.

❽ To assemble, set the table legs as an upright U and glue the tabletop, centered, on top (fig. 37.8). Let dry.

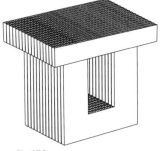

Fig. 37.8

WHAT YOU NEED

- Piece of ¾"-thick plywood or MDF, cut to fit the width of your bed frame and extend at least 2' above the bed
- Tape measure
- Ruler
- Craft knife
- Self-healing cutting mat
- Wallpaper roll
- Large paintbrush
- Wallpaper paste
- Brayer
- Small scissors
- Pencil
- Small scraps of paper (at least 1" square) in several different colors
- Small paintbrush

38 | Off-the-Wall Headboard

LEVEL ⊗ ⊗ ⊗ ⊗ ⊗

Do you have champagne taste on a beer budget? Join the club. For years I lived a headboard-free existence and dreamed of the day when I could afford a fancy bed, until I realized I could just make my own and get on with my life! With just a sheet of plywood or MDF, a roll of wallpaper, some paper scraps, and elbow grease, you too can live the dream. *Note:* Applying wallpaper can sometimes be a two-person job, so go ahead and recruit a buddy.

— ⊹ —

① Measure the width (x) and height (y) of the plywood headboard (fig. 38.1).

Fig. 38.1

② Use the ruler, craft knife, and cutting mat to cut a piece of wallpaper equal to x + 7".

③ Use the large brush to coat the top of the headboard with wallpaper paste. Horizontally apply the piece of wallpaper so that the long edge of the wallpaper extends 4" beyond the top edge of the headboard and the side edges extend 3½" at either side. Make

sure the wallpaper goes on evenly, and smooth the wallpaper with a brayer (fig. 38.3).

④ Brush wallpaper paste along each of the side edges and a few inches along the back of the headboard. Fold the wallpaper over the sides, then smooth with a brayer (fig. 38.4).

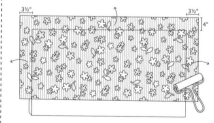

Fig. 38.3–4

⑤ Fold in the top corners of the wallpaper as if you were wrapping a present, brush the top few inches

of the back of the headboard with wallpaper paste, and wrap the wallpaper around the top edge to the back of the headboard. Smooth with a brayer (fig. 38.5).

Fig. 38.5

6 For the second row of wallpaper, unroll a piece, matching up the pattern with the bottom edge of the first piece, and use a craft knife to cut it equal in length to the first (fig. 38.6). *Note:* You may need to roll out more paper in order to match up the pattern. Just trim the excess wallpaper and save it for another project.

7 Brush the headboard with wallpaper paste where the second row will be applied (fig. 38.7). Press the second piece so it butts up against but doesn't overlap the bottom edge of the first piece.

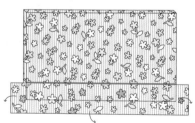

Fig. 38.6–7

8 Repeat step 4 to wrap the sides of the wallpaper around the headboard. If necessary, repeat steps 6 and 7 until the headboard is covered. *Note:* No wallpaper is needed to wrap around the bottom, since it won't be visible.

9 Use scissors to cut a small piece of wallpaper from the roll or select a leftover scrap. Cut out some of the details of the wallpaper pattern to use as a template (fig. 38.9).

Fig. 38.9

10 Use the pencil to trace the shapes onto additional scraps of paper and cut them out (fig. 38.10).

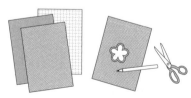

Fig. 38.10

11 Brush the back of each piece with wallpaper paste and the small brush. Arrange and press them onto the wallpapered headboard as desired: Apply them in an even pattern, scatter them across the board, or cluster them into one corner or side so they "spray" out across the board (fig. 38.11). Let dry completely.

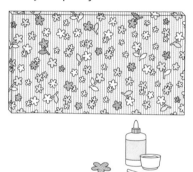

Fig. 38.11

VARIATION

If you already have a plain headboard that you'd like to cover, just measure the height, width, and depth and adapt the instructions accordingly. Note: A plain old IKEA Malm headboard can be used to create stunning results!

Kusudama *Headband*, page 114

That's a Wrap Bangle, page 103

CHAPTER

four

PAPER'S IN
FASHION

39 | It's Classified Necklace

WHAT YOU NEED

. . . .

- *Yellow pages book*
- *Ruler*
- *Craft knife*
- *Self-healing cutting mat*
- *Toothpicks*
- *Small paintbrush*
- *White glue*
- *Embroidery floss*
- *Scissors*

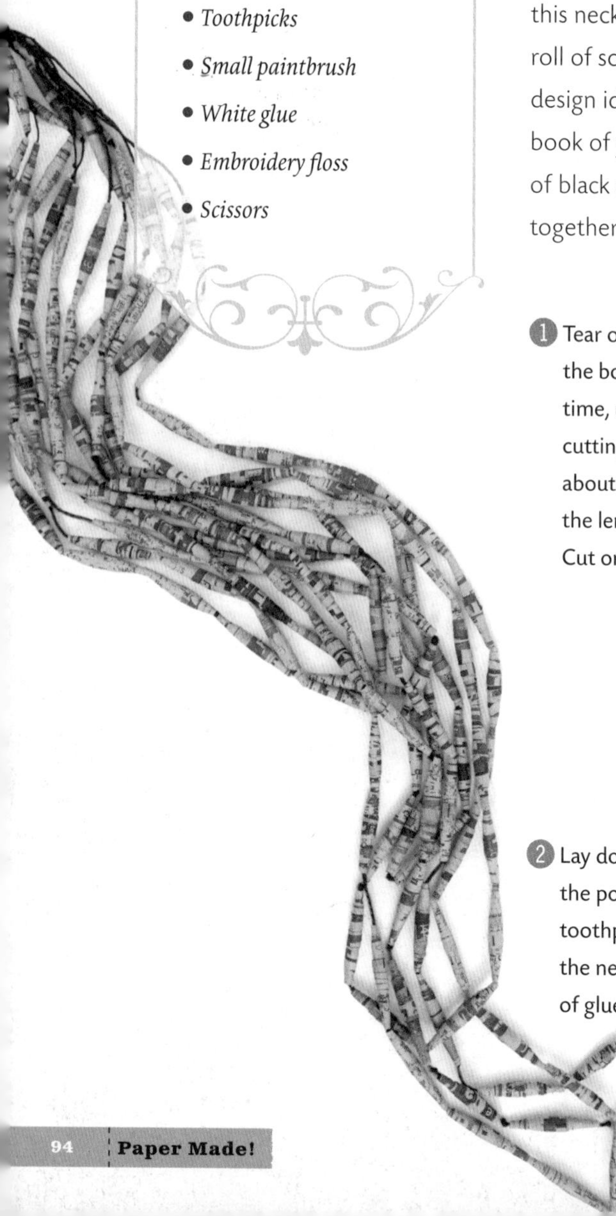

LEVEL ✪ ✪ ✪ ✖ ✖

You may remember making paper beads when you were in grade school. While the technique for this project is the same, the delicate multiple strands and graphic monochromatic tones of this necklace make for a truly grown-up statement piece. All it takes is a roll of scrap paper and, magically, you have a bead. Sometimes the best design ideas come from the most humble materials: In this case, an old book of yellow pages on our front stoop inspired me with its graphic pops of black and red. This necklace requires a whole lot of beads but comes together very quickly in the end.

1 Tear out about twenty pages from the book. Working one page at a time, use a ruler, craft knife, and cutting mat to cut triangular strips about 1½" at one end and running the length of the page (fig. 39.1). Cut one hundred strips.

Fig. 39.1

2 Lay down one strip of paper with the point away from you. Place a toothpick ½" from and parallel to the near end. Brush a small amount of glue along the edge, fold it 1" around the toothpick, and press it to the paper, forming a loop and securing the end of the paper to itself, not to the toothpick (fig. 39.2).

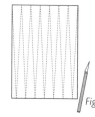

Fig. 39.2

3 With the toothpick at the top of the loop, tightly roll the paper toward the pointed end, applying a small amount of glue every two or three rolls to secure (fig. 39.3).

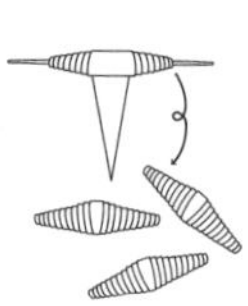

Fig. 39.3

4 At the end, brush glue over the whole bead, remove the toothpick, and let dry for half an hour. Repeat to make 108 more beads.

5 Cut five pieces of embroidery floss to the following measurements: 26", 32", 36", 44", and 48".

6 Make a knot 2" from one end of the 26" floss. Thread one paper bead onto the other end and slide it down to meet the double knot. Make a knot above the bead to secure it. Add fifteen more beads in this manner, until you reach the end of the floss. Make a knot at the end (fig. 39.6).

Fig. 39.6

7 Repeat step 6 for the remaining four lengths of floss, adding eighteen beads on the 32" floss, twenty-two beads on the 36" floss, twenty-five beads on the 44" floss, and twenty-eight beads on the 48" floss.

8 Lay the shortest strand of beads on a flat surface and fold it gently in half to make an arc. One at a time, lay the other four lengths of beaded floss in ascending

Fig. 39.8

order outside the first strand (fig. 39.8).

9 Line up and gather all the ends from both sides of the strands and tie them in a knot (fig. 39.9).

Fig. 39.9

❖

Paper Dolls

Brazilian artist Jum Nakao caused quite a stir at the 2004 São Paulo Fashion Week when he sent his models down the runway in nothing but paper. It took 150 people more than 180 hours of work to fold, sculpt, and laser-cut one ton of paper to create. Imagine the audience's surprise when, at the end of the show, the models disrobed and tore apart their dresses at the behest of the designer!

WHAT YOU NEED

- Access to a computer with a printer and paper
- Chain templates A and B*
- Pencil
- Incomplete deck of cards (or about 12 cards)
- Craft knife
- Self-healing cutting mat
- White glue
- Water
- Small foam brush
- Acrylic sealer (optional)
- Scissors
- Grosgrain ribbon (1 yard, ½" or ¾" wide)
- E6000 glue

* Download at workman.com/papermade

40 | Queen of Hearts Necklace

LEVEL ⊗ ⊗ ⊗ ⊗ ⊗

Another partial deck of cards found at a thrift store. What to do? Cards always get me thinking about Alice and her marvelous adventures in Wonderland, so I thought, *Why not make a necklace fit for a queen?*

1. Print the chain templates A and B and cut them out using the craft knife and cutting mat.

2. With a pencil, trace template A onto the cards eleven times (fig. 40.2).

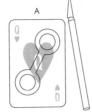

Fig. 40.2

3. Use the craft knife and cutting mat to cut around the traced A pieces. Lining up the circles, fold all the pieces in half, creasing them, and then unfold them (fig. 40.3).

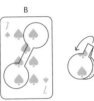

Fig. 40.3

4. Repeat steps 2 and 3 to create five pieces from template B (fig. 40.4).

Fig. 40.4

5. To complete the first link of the chain, fold one A piece along the crease. Slide one ring of the next A piece through the ring of the first, and fold it on the crease (fig. 40.5).

Fig. 40.5

6. Repeat step 5 to add the remaining A pieces to the chain (fig. 40.6).

Fig. 40.6

7. Lay the chain in an arc. Locate the three center pieces in the chain (counting from one end, they should be in positions 5, 6, and 7). Select a B piece, slide one circle through link 5, and then fold it on the crease. Repeat with two more B pieces on links 6 and 7, then glue the inside of each circle to its match to secure each bauble onto the chain (fig. 40.7).

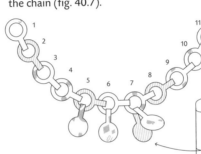

Fig. 40.7

8. Attach a B piece to one end of the chain by sliding one circle through the chain, and fold it on the crease. Repeat with another B piece on the other end of the chain (fig. 40.8).

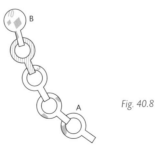

Fig. 40.8

9. To seal, mix up a diluted glue solution of three parts white glue and one part water, and brush a coat over the whole necklace. (*Optional:* Spray the front and back of the chain with acrylic sealer in a well-ventilated area.) Let dry.

10. Cut the ribbon in half. Squeeze a dot of E6000 glue on the inside of the circles of the B piece at the end of the necklace. Sandwich the end of one piece of ribbon in between those circles (fig. 40.10). Repeat with the second piece of ribbon and the B piece at the other end of the necklace. Let dry.

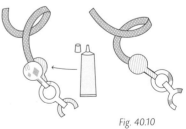

Fig. 40.10

11. To wear, tie the ribbon ends at the back of the neck.

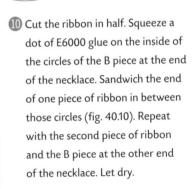

41 | Gallerina Necklace

LEVEL ✪ ✪ ✪ ✪ ⊗

WHAT YOU NEED

- *Access to a computer with a printer and paper*
- *Shape templates**
- *Scissors*
- *Pencil*
- *Small foam brush*
- *White glue*
- *Heavy cardboard (the back cover of a pad of drawing paper works well)*
- *Craft knife*
- *Self-healing cutting mat*
- *12 to 15 paint chips (in several different colors)*
- *Awl*
- *Hammer*
- *Acrylic sealer (optional)*
- *Embroidery or tapestry needle with an eye large enough for linen thread*
- *Waxed linen thread*

Wearing this necklace is like putting a piece of modern art around your neck. I love the rich saturated colors of the paint chips and the way the shapes hang gracefully off simple waxed linen thread. I've provided you with some basic shape templates to get you started, but here the design assembly is mostly left up to you because, like all good art, this necklace should be one of a kind.

1. Print the diamond, square, and teardrop templates, and cut them out using scissors.

2. Trace the templates onto the backs of the paint chips and cut out the shapes. Then brush the back of the paint chip shapes with glue and press them onto the cardboard. Let dry.

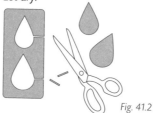

Fig. 41.2

3. Use the craft knife and cutting mat to carefully cut out the shapes from the cardboard (fig. 41.3).

Fig. 41.3

4. Select one cardboard shape and brush the back with glue. Press it against the back of another paint chip (fig. 41.4). Let dry.

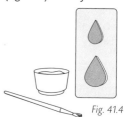

Fig. 41.4

5. Trim away the edges of the paint chip with the craft knife. Repeat with the remaining cardboard shapes (fig. 41.5).

Fig. 41.5

* Download at workman.com/papermade

6 Use the awl and a hammer to neatly pierce small holes 3/8" from the edges of the shapes as indicated in the illustration (fig. 41.6).

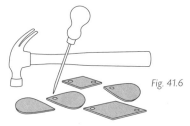

Fig. 41.6

7 Organize the shapes in the order in which you'd like them to appear in the necklace (fig. 41.7). *Optional:* Spray the front, back, and sides of the shapes with an acrylic sealer and let dry. Repeat step 6 to remove any sealer from the holes.

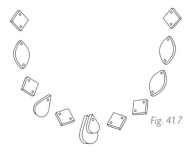

Fig. 41.7

8 Stand in front of a mirror and, without cutting the thread, drape some around your neck to determine the desired length of the necklace, making sure the thread length will fit over your head. Then cut a piece of thread that is twice the desired length of the necklace.

9 Use a needle and thread to slide the first shape onto the necklace. Make a knot around the edge of the shape to secure it in place, then pass the needle through the second hole on the shape and make another knot (fig. 41.9a). For the droplet shape, slide it on and knot it only at the top (fig. 41.9b). Continue adding shapes, spacing them between 1/4" to 1 1/2" apart, or as desired.

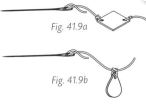

Fig. 41.9a

Fig. 41.9b

10 Try on the necklace again and adjust it to the desired length. Knot the ends of the thread together and trim the excess (fig. 41.10).

Fig. 41.10

Great Scott!

In 1966, for just one dollar, the Scott Paper Company would send you a shapeless paper dress that you could customize, plus a bevy of Scott coupons. While the dress was intended as a marketing tool, Scott was surprised that women went crazy for the idea. Soon manufacturers began churning out everything from paper bell-bottom suits to paper wedding dresses and hostess gowns that matched your party napkins and tablecloths. It was a time of new inventions and new ideas, and everyone seemed excited about what the future could hold. "After all," an article in *Life* magazine stated, "who is going to do laundry in space?"

- Hardcover book that's past its prime (size as desired)

- Craft knife

- Ruler

- Cotton fabric (¼ to ½ yard, depending on the size of your book)

- Scissors

- Iron

- Pencil

- White scrap paper

- Straight pins

- Access to a sewing machine (threaded with color to match fabric)

- Fabric glue

- Purse handles

- Grosgrain ribbon (½ yard, 1" to 1½" wide)

42 | Hardcover Book Bag

LEVEL ⊗ ⊗ ⊗ ⊗ ⊗

I once happened upon a big box of books in the trash room of my building. The pages of the books were somewhat damaged—yellowed and water-stained—but the covers were still in pretty good shape. One, a big old dictionary, was destined to become this handbag—or should I say book bag?

1 Use the craft knife to separate the pages from the book cover, taking care not to cut through the spine (fig. 42.1).

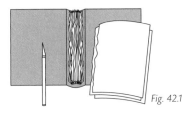

Fig. 42.1

2 Lay the book cover flat and measure the width (a) and height (b). Add 1" to both measurements to get x and y (fig. 42.2).

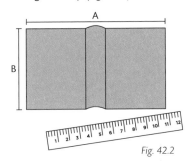

Fig. 42.2

3 Measure and cut a piece of the fabric to x and y. Iron a ½" seam allowance on all sides of the piece of fabric and set it aside (fig. 42.3).

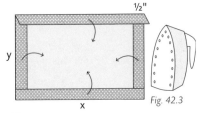

Fig. 42.3

4 Stand up the open cover (at approximately a 45-degree angle) and use a pencil to trace around the outside of the cover onto a piece of scrap paper. Draw a straight line connecting the open ends to form a triangular shape (fig. 42.4).

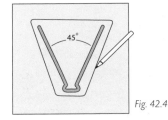

Fig. 42.4

5 Add ½" on all sides to the traced pattern piece, and cut it out (fig. 42.5).

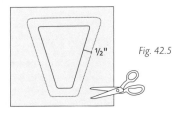

Fig. 42.5

6 Fold the pattern piece in half and cut down the middle (fig. 42.6).

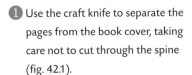

Fig. 42.6

7 Fold a piece of fabric right sides together and pin the new pattern piece to the center of the fabric. Add ½" to the straight edge of the pattern, and cut through both layers of fabric (fig. 42.7).

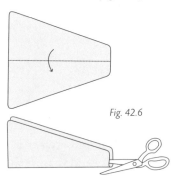

Fig. 42.7

8 With both pieces still right sides together, sew just down the straight edge of the shape with a ½" seam allowance (fig. 42.8).

Fig. 42.8

9 Repeat steps 7 and 8. You should have two triangle-esque shapes. Press open the seams (fig. 42.9).

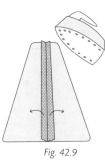

Fig. 42.9

10 Pin these triangle shapes to a piece of fabric right sides down, and cut out. Now you should have four triangle pieces, two with seams down the middle and two without.

11 Pin a seamed and unseamed triangle right sides together. Sew around all edges of the piece, leaving a 2" opening at the bottom for turning (fig. 42.11). Repeat for the other two triangles.

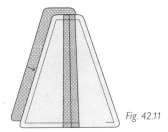

Fig. 42.11

12 Trim the excess fabric from the seams and turn both triangles right sides out. Press, then use a few dots of fabric glue to close the openings on both triangles.

13 Lay the book cover flat again and place one purse handle centered at the left and right edges. Cut four 4" pieces of ribbon. Thread through the handles and secure them to the inside of the book cover with fabric glue (fig. 42.13).

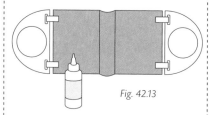

Fig. 42.13

14 Place the narrow ends of each triangle piece ½" into the spine of the book. Glue in place (fig. 42.14). Let dry for a few minutes.

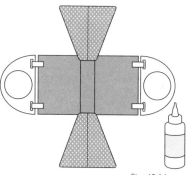

Fig. 42.14

15 Now glue one long edge of the triangle pieces to one long edge of the book cover, about ½" in from the edge of the cover (fig. 42.15). Let dry for a few minutes.

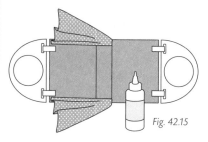

Fig. 42.15

16 On the side where the triangles are connected to the book cover, glue the lining in place, making sure it covers the edges of the triangle pieces (fig. 42.16). Let dry for a few minutes.

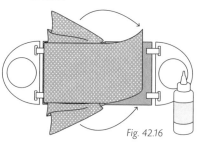

Fig. 42.16

17 Glue the other long edge of the triangles to the other long edges of the book cover, about ½" in from the edge of the cover. Let dry for a few minutes, then attach the lining to the other side of the book cover (fig. 42.17). Let the whole piece dry.

Fig. 42.17

43 That's a Wrap Bangle

LEVEL ❌ ⊗ ⊗ ⊗ ⊗

This is one of the easiest paper projects, and the results are stunning. Paper-wrapped bangles in boutiques go for a pretty penny, but you can make your own for a few bucks. These are so quick to make that you could start this project before dinner and have a new accessory for your out-on-the-town outfit that night.

1. Use the ruler, craft knife, and cutting mat to cut ½"-wide strips of paper (fig. 43.1).

Fig. 43.1

2. Brush decoupage medium onto one end of a paper strip and press it along the inside of the bangle to secure it (fig. 43.2).

Fig. 43.2

3. Brush the rest of the bangle with decoupage medium and start wrapping the paper strip around the bangle, easing the paper strip as you wrap so it lies flat against the bangle (fig. 43.3).

Fig. 43.3

4. Continue wrapping the paper strip until you have covered the entire bangle or you run out of paper. If you reach the end of the paper strip, trim it so the end is hidden on the inside of the bangle and apply decoupage medium to it. Then start another paper strip, overlapping the end of the first on the inside of the bangle. Let dry.

5. Brush the entire bangle with two coats of decoupage medium to seal, allowing for drying time in between each coat.

WHAT YOU NEED

(makes 1 bangle)

- Ruler
- Craft knife
- Self-healing cutting mat
- Scraps of wallpaper or wrapping paper
- Small foam brush
- Decoupage medium
- Plastic or wood bangle

WHAT YOU NEED
· ·

- 16 to 20 gum wrappers
  (18 gum wrappers make
  a 7" to 8" bracelet)

- Ruler

44 | I Want Candy Bracelet

LEVEL ✖ ✖ ✖ ✖ ✖

This bracelet has the distinction of requiring the fewest materials of any project in this chapter, so it is the perfect to-go project. Once you get the hang of the technique, you can make the chains while watching a movie, hanging out with friends, sitting in the park, riding a bus . . . pretty much anywhere!

1 Open a gum wrapper and smooth it out. Fold it in half lengthwise and crease.

2 Use the ruler to tear the wrapper in half along the crease (fig. 44.2). Set aside one half.

Fig. 44.2

3 Lay the paper piece right side down. Fold it in half lengthwise and open it up. Fold the side edges in to meet the center fold (fig. 44.3).

Fig. 44.3

4 Fold the piece in half lengthwise and crease (fig. 44.4).

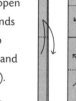

Fig. 44.4

5 Fold the piece in half widthwise and open it up. Fold the ends of the strip in to the middle fold and crease (fig. 44.5).

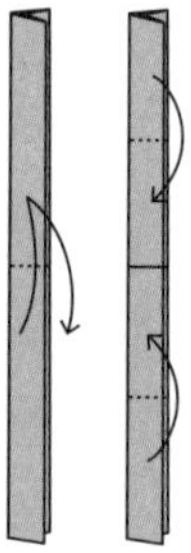

Fig. 44.5

6 Fold the piece in half widthwise again to complete the first chain link (fig. 44.6).

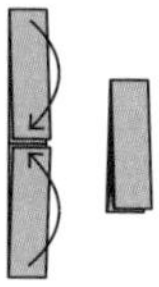

Fig. 44.6

7 Repeat steps 3 through 6 with the second half of the gum wrapper. Then repeat steps 1 through 6 with the remaining gum wrappers.

8 To begin the chain, slide the prongs of one link (A) into the slots of a second link (B) and pull taut (fig. 44.8). Together, connected links A and B will look like a V.

Fig. 44.8

9 Hold the connected links A and B in the V shape with one hand, and slide the prongs of the link into the slots of the link on one side of the V (fig. 44.9).

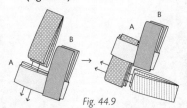

Fig. 44.9

10 Keep adding links until you have made a chain that, when closed, will slide easily on and off your wrist. To connect the last link, unfold the last two folds you made in step 6 and insert the longer prongs into the slots of the link at the other end of the chain (fig. 44.10).

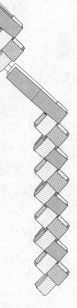

Fig. 44.10

11 Gently slide the two bracelet ends together. Refold and tuck the prongs of the long V into the slots on the other side of the bracelet (the reverse action of what you were doing before) (fig. 44.11).

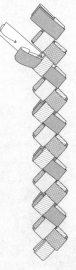

Fig. 44.11

VARIATION

If you want a wider bracelet, try stitching two or more bracelets together. Stack them so that all the pieces lock in together, and use a needle threaded with fishing line to connect them from the inside of the bracelet. If you're feeling brave, tackle a gum wrapper purse using the same technique!

WHAT YOU NEED

- *Lightweight, noncorrugated cardboard (a food packaging box works well)*
- *Pencil*
- *Scissors*
- *Hammer*
- *Awl*
- *Elastic thread*
- *Needle*
- *4 wooden beads*
- *Small paintbrush (optional)*
- *Gold-leaf paint (optional)*

45 | **Paper Chips Bracelet**

LEVEL ⊗ ⊗ ⊗ ⊗ ⊗

Once upon a time, I was browsing in a fancy boutique in London and spied some gorgeous necklaces made from hundreds of stacked cardboard circles. The design was beautiful, but the price tag was just hideous. Inspired by both the design and that terrifying number on the tag, I set about making my own version the moment I got home. The cutting part of this DIY bracelet takes the most time, but it's easy work, and the result is, well, London boutique–worthy.

---

1 Trace and cut seventy-five 1½" circles from cardboard. Cut each circle in half.

2 Stack ten half circles and, using the hammer and awl, make two holes through each half circle about ¼" from the straight edge and ¼" from each side (fig. 45.2). Repeat with the remaining half circles.

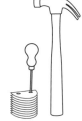

Fig. 45.2

3 Cut two 20" pieces of elastic thread. Thread one piece onto a needle.

4 Poke the needle through all the holes on one side of the half circles. Center the half circles on the string (fig. 45.4).

Fig. 45.4

5 Thread the needle with the second piece of thread and poke it through all the holes on the opposite side of the half circles. Center them on the thread (fig. 45.5).

Fig. 45.5

6 Thread a wooden bead onto one of the elastic thread ends (fig. 45.6).

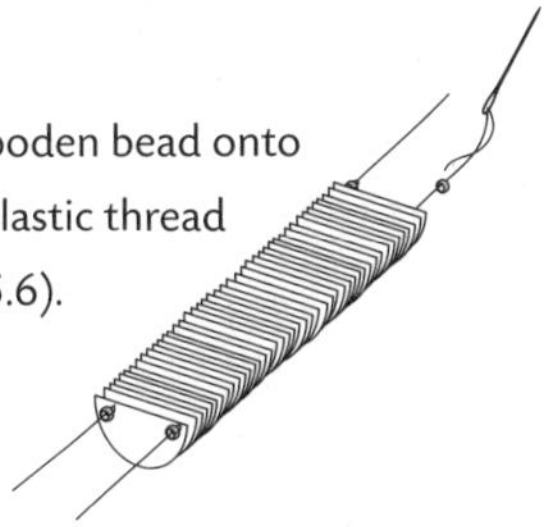

Fig. 45.6

7 Bring the needle around the bead and back through the hole to secure it. Repeat for the second wooden bead and adjacent thread end (fig. 45.7).

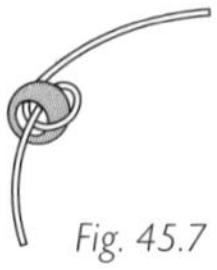

Fig. 45.7

8 Repeat step 7 for the remaining two wooden beads and the two opposite thread ends (fig. 45.8).

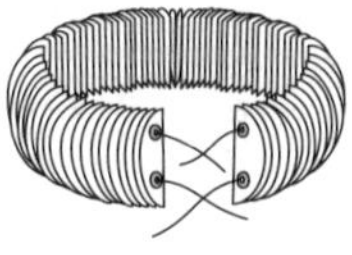

Fig. 45.8

9 Tie the corresponding thread ends tightly together in two square knots (fig. 45.9). *Optional:* Brush gold-leaf paint on the edges of the half circles.

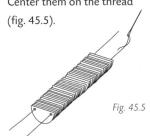

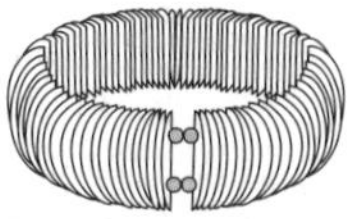

Fig. 45.9

46 | Blooms and Berries Barrettes

LEVEL ⊗ ⊗ ⊗ ⊗ ⊗

Quilling is a paper crafting technique that dates back to the Renaissance. Once a hobby of the wealthy, presumably because they had time on their hands, it's much more a craft of the people, because it requires very few materials or special tools. These sweet little barrettes are a good introduction to the art of quilling because they take less than an hour to make.

WHAT YOU NEED

• *Ruler*

• *Craft knife*

• *Self-healing cutting mat*

• *Scraps of paper (at least 8" × 16") in different colors and patterns*

• *Toothpick*

• *Small paintbrush*

• *Decoupage medium*

• *Bobby pins*

• *E6000 glue*

• *Acrylic sealer (optional)*

To make the flower barrette

1 Use the ruler, craft knife, and cutting mat to cut six ¼" × 16" paper strips for the petals of the flower. Cut one ¼" × 12" strip for the flower center. Then cut two 1" circles from the paper you used for the petals (fig. 46.1).

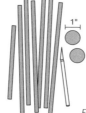

Fig. 46.1

2 For one petal, start by rolling the paper tightly around the toothpick (fig. 46.2). Continue to roll the paper strip until you reach the end. Slide the paper off the toothpick and let the roll unravel slightly.

Pinch two sides of the circular coil to make an approximately 1"-long petal shape. Adhere the end in place with decoupage medium and a brush and apply a little bit of medium to the center of the petal just on the underside (fig. 46.2). Repeat with the five remaining petal strips.

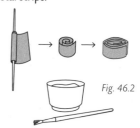

Fig. 46.2

3 For the center, tightly roll the strip onto a toothpick, secure the ends with decoupage medium, and gently slide the roll off the toothpick to dry (fig. 46.3).

Fig. 46.3

4 With the glued undersides facing down, arrange the six petals together to form a flower. Brush the sides of the petals with decoupage medium and gently press them together to secure (fig. 46.4). Let dry.

Fig. 46.4

5 Apply decoupage medium to the wrong side of one of the 1" paper circles and press it, centered, onto the petal cluster (fig. 46.5). Let dry. Brush the bottom of the flower center from step 3 with decoupage medium and press it to the 1" paper circle. Let dry.

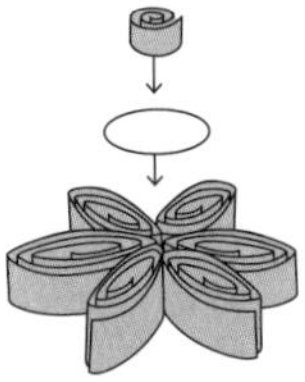

Fig. 46.5

6 Dot the top of a bobby pin with E6000 glue and press it against the back of the flower. Let dry, and then glue the second 1" circle over the bobby pin (fig 46.6). Let dry.

Fig. 46.6

To make the berry barrette

7 Cut two 2¼" × 16" strips of paper for the leaves. Cut two ¼" × 12" strips and one ¼" × 6" strip for the berries.

8 Make the leaves the way you made the flower petals in step 2.

9 Make the berries the way you made the flower center in step 3.

10 Brush the sides of the berries with decoupage medium and press them together in a cluster (fig. 46.10). Let dry.

Fig. 46.10

11 Brush the sides of the leaves with decoupage medium and press them together and then to the berries (fig. 46.11). Let dry.

Fig. 46.11

12 Dot the tip of a bobby pin with E6000 glue and adhere to the back of the berries. Cut a small oblong shape from the same paper you used to cut the leaves and glue it over the bobby pin (fig. 46.12).

Fig. 46.12

13 Brush a coat of decoupage medium over the leaves and berries to seal them. *Optional:* Or spray with a coat of acrylic sealer in a well-ventilated area. Let dry (fig. 46.13).

Fig. 46.13

❀
Greeking Out

At first glance, artist Siba Sahabi's work resembles delicate ceramic vessels and vases (www.sibasahabi.com). Viewers might think Sahabi was following in the tradition of Greek pottery until they take a closer look: Instead of a potter's wheel, Sahabi works with strips of paper, carefully rolled and shaped to look just like the real thing.

- Ruler
- Craft knife
- Self-healing cutting mat
- Small scraps of paper (at least 2" × 2") in three different colors or patterns
- Small paintbrush
- Decoupage medium
- 2 small beads
- 2 head pins (2")
- E6000 glue
- 2 jump rings (6mm)
- Round-nose pliers
- 2 earring wires
- Acrylic sealer (optional)

47 | Paper Trail Earrings

LEVEL ✪ ✪ ✪ ⊗ ⊗

The more paper crafting you do, the more little scraps of paper you will have. And the more scraps of paper you will have, the more pairs of these earrings you can make! These accessories benefit from a diverse collection of found papers—each color, texture, and pattern peeks out over the next in brilliant harmony.

1. Use the ruler, craft knife, and cutting mat to cut six 2" squares from the paper (fig. 47.1).

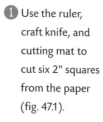

Fig. 47.1

2. Select a paper square and lay it right side down, rotated so it looks like a diamond.

3. Curl the left and right points together to make a cone (fig. 47.3). Brush a line of decoupage medium on the overlapping edges to hold the cone's shape. Leave a *tiny* hole at the top.

Fig. 47.3

4. Repeat step 4 with five more paper squares to make five more cones. Stack them, one inside the other (fig. 47.4).

Fig. 47.4

5. Slide a bead onto one of the head pins (fig. 47.5).

Fig. 47.5

6. Dot the bead with E6000 glue and insert the head pin through the bottom of the stacked cones (fig. 47.6). (The head pin should be sticking out of the top.)

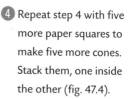

Fig. 47.6

7 Slide a jump ring over that end of the head pin. Use the pliers to make a small loop out of the end of the head pin that encloses the jump ring (fig. 47.7). Twist the end of the pin around itself to secure.

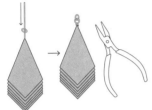

Fig. 47.7

8 Open an earring wire with the pliers and slide it onto the jump ring. Close the jump ring (fig. 47.8).

Fig. 47.8

9 Repeat steps 1 through 8 to make the second earring.

10 To seal, brush a coat of decoupage medium over the earrings. *Optional:* Or spray with a coat of acrylic sealer in a well-ventilated area. Let dry.

- 1" scalloped round hole punch

- Scraps of card stock in different colors (enough to make forty-eight 1"-diameter circles)

- Small paintbrush

- White glue

- 2 head pins (2½")

- 2 small wood beads

- Wire cutters

- Round-nose pliers

- 2 eye pins (2½")

- 2 jump rings (6 mm)

- 2 earring wires

- Flat-nose pliers

48 | Carousel Ride Earrings

LEVEL ⊗ ⊗ ⊗ ⊗ ⊗

These earrings conjure the sights, the smells, and the whimsy of a childhood summer carnival: cotton candy, Ferris wheels, snow cones, and carousel rides—pure magic and color. These vibrant earrings are for kids of all ages.

---

① Punch out forty-eight scalloped circles from the card stock scraps. Then fold all forty-eight circles in half (fig. 48.1).

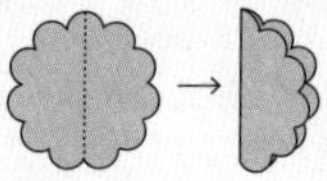

Fig. 48.1

② Separate twelve folded half circles. Select one and brush glue onto one half of the outside. Press it against the outside of a second half circle (fig. 48.2).

Fig. 48.2

③ Repeat step 2 to glue each of the remaining ten half circles to the next to create an orb-shaped bead. Finish the bead by gluing the last half circle to the first (fig. 48.3).

Fig. 48.3

④ Repeat steps 2 and 3 to make three more beads. Let dry completely.

⑤ Select one head pin and slide a wood bead onto it, followed by one of the four paper beads (fig. 48.5). Use wire cutters to trim the end of the head pin to ½" above the bead.

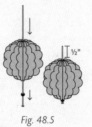

Fig. 48.5

⑥ Use the round-nose pliers to start bending the wire to make a loop. Before closing the loop, slide an eye pin onto it (fig. 48.6).

Fig. 48.6

⑦ Slide a paper bead onto the eye pin. Trim the end of the eye pin to ½" above the bead. Use the round-nose pliers to bend the wire to make a loop (fig. 48.7).

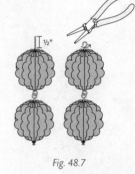

Fig. 48.7

⑧ Open a jump ring with the flat-nose pliers and slide it onto the loop of the top of the eye pin. Then slip an earring wire onto the jump ring and close it (fig. 48.8).

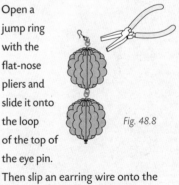

Fig. 48.8

⑨ Repeat steps 5 through 8 to complete the second earring.

WHAT YOU NEED

....

- *Ruler*

- *Craft knife*

- *Self-healing cutting mat*

- *Scraps of paper (at least 3" square) in a few different colors and patterns*

- *Small foam brush*

- *Decoupage medium*

- *Strips of paper (to wrap the headband)*

- *Scissors*

- *White glue*

- *Access to a sewing machine and thread (optional)*

- *Hot glue gun and glue*

- *Acrylic sealer (optional)*

49 | *Kusudama* Headband

LEVEL ✪ ✪ ✪ ✪ ○

The Japanese *kusudama,* or medicine ball, is a paper ball made out of multiple identical origami shapes glued together. Traditionally, they were used to hold incense or potpourri, but today they are widely made as decoration or gifts. The origami flowers that are combined to create a *kusudama* are pretty gorgeous on their own, so I scavenged some scrap gift wrap and old book pages to give them the spotlight on this headband.

❶ Use the ruler, craft knife, and cutting mat to cut five 3" paper squares and five 2½" paper squares.

❷ Select one 3" square and lay it right side down, oriented with points facing out like a diamond shape. Fold the bottom point up to meet the top, forming a triangle shape (fig. 49.2).

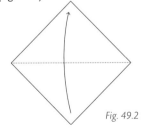

Fig. 49.2

❸ Fold the left and right points up to meet the top, forming another diamond shape (fig. 49.3).

Fig. 49.3

❹ Fold the same points down so that the inside folded edge lines up with the outside folded edge (fig. 49.4).

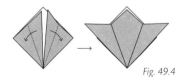

Fig. 49.4

❺ Open the flaps made in step 4 and flatten them (fig. 49.5).

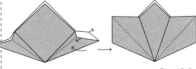

Fig. 49.5

❻ Fold the two top side triangles down (fig. 49.6).

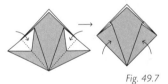

Fig. 49.6

❼ Fold the outer flaps in again to form a diamond shape (fig. 49.7).

Fig. 49.7

❽ Curl the lower left and right edges together to form a cone (fig. 49.8). Brush decoupage medium along the flaps and secure them to complete one flower petal.

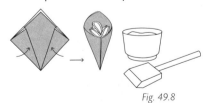

Fig. 49.8

9 Repeat steps 2 through 8 to create four more petals. Apply decoupage medium generously along each petal seam and bundle them together to make a flower (fig. 49.9).

Fig. 49.9

10 Repeat steps 2 through 9 with the 2½" squares to make a smaller flower.

11 Snip about 1" from the pointed backs of the flowers and set the flowers aside (fig. 49.11).

1"

Fig. 49.11

12 Cut two ¼" × 6" strips of paper. Roll one strip tightly around a pencil and glue the end to the coil. Slide the coil off the pencil and allow it to unravel at the center. Then hot glue the coil to the center of the large flower. Repeat with the second strip and glue it to the smaller flower.

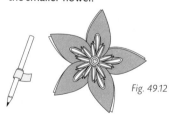

Fig. 49.12

13 Cut about eighteen ⅛" × 8" strips of paper.

14 Brush decoupage medium on one end of the headband and start wrapping the end of a paper strip tightly and evenly around the band (fig. 49.14). Continue brushing with medium and wrapping strips until the band is covered.

Fig. 49.14

15 To seal, brush decoupage medium over the headband. Let dry.

16 Fold some of the scrap paper in half and cut seven 1½"-long leaf shapes through both layers (fig. 49.16). Match the shapes from the two layers and glue them together with white glue to make double-sided leaves. *Optional:* Stitch the leaves together along the center using a sewing machine and matching thread.

Fig. 49.16

17 Squeeze dots of hot glue slightly off-center along the outside of the headband, and attach the leaves in clusters (fig. 49.17).

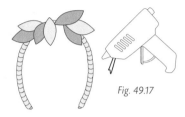

Fig. 49.17

18 Hot glue the back of the flowers on top of the leaves (fig. 49.18).

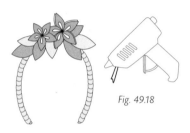

Fig. 49.18

19 Brush a coat of the decoupage medium over the entire headband to seal it. *Optional:* Or spray with a coat of acrylic sealer in a well-ventilated area. Let dry.

50 | **Paper Economy Wallet**

LEVEL ⊗ ⊗ ⊗ ⊗ ⊗

Money may be tight, but you still need a stylish wallet to stash the cash you have! This project uses just one waterproof envelope to make an unbelievably durable wallet. But that's not even the best part: The material is just as easy to print on as standard copy paper, so you can customize your wallet with artwork, book pages, or maps. The sample here includes illustrations from a very old Girl Scout manual—far too precious to cut up, but very handy for artistic inspiration!

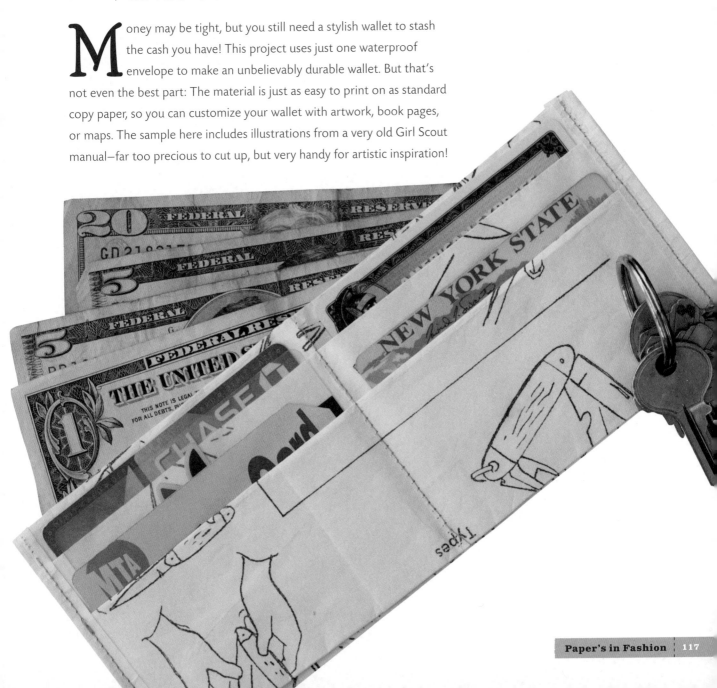

WHAT YOU NEED
· · · · · · · · · · · · · · · · · · · ·

- *Waterproof envelope (9" × 12"), such as Tyvek*

- *Ruler*

- *Craft knife*

- *Self-healing cutting mat*

- *Access to a scanner, computer, photo editing program, and printer*

- *Artwork or book pages to scan onto the envelope (a completely abstract pattern or block of words work best)*

- *Pencil*

- *Access to a sewing machine (with vinyl or leather sewing needle), threaded with contrasting thread*

1 Use the ruler, craft knife, and cutting mat to square off the sides and bottom of the envelope to create two 8½" × 11" sheets of paper (fig. 50.1).

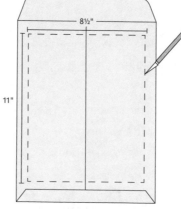

Fig. 50.1

2 Scan the artwork or book pages and use a photo editing program to enlarge the artwork to 8½" × 11".

3 Feed one of the sheets into the printer and print the artwork onto the page (sheet A) (fig. 50.3).

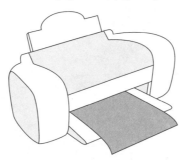

Fig. 50.3

4 Measure and cut sheet A to 8" × 8½" (fig. 50.4).

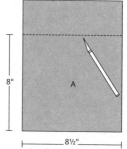

Fig. 50.4

5 Orient sheet A right side up and fold the two shorter sides ¼" toward the center (fig. 50.5).

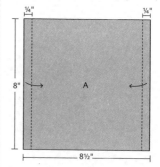

Fig. 50.5

6 Flip the sheet over, right side down, oriented so the folded seams are to the left and the right. Use the ruler and pencil to measure and mark a horizontal line 1" from the top and bottom of the sheet. Fold along those lines and crease. Then fold the sheet in half lengthwise and crease (fig 50.6).

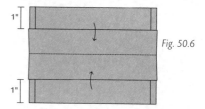

Fig. 50.6

7 Fold the piece in half widthwise, crease, and set it aside (fig 50.7).

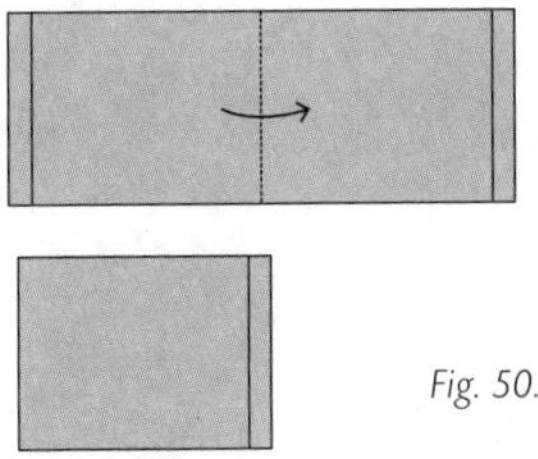

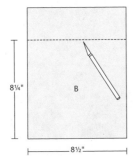

Fig. 50.7

8 Select the second sheet (sheet B) and cut it to 8½" × 8¼" (fig. 50.8).

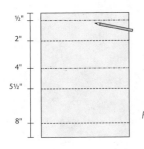

8¼"

B

8½"

Fig. 50.8

9 Orient sheet B so that the short sides are at the top and bottom. Measure and mark horizontal lines from the top of the page at ½", 2", 4", 5½", and 8" (fig. 50.9).

½"
2"
4"
5½"
8"

Fig. 50.9

10 Mountain fold at the ½" mark, valley fold at 2", mountain fold at 4", and valley fold at 5½" and 8", then crease (fig. 50.10).

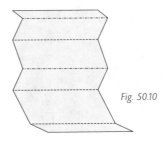

Fig. 50.10

11 Fold up sheet B, following the creases.

12 Fold B in half widthwise to crease, and unfold. Use the sewing machine to stitch along the crease line (fig. 50.12).

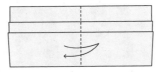

Fig. 50.12

13 Tuck the sides of piece B into the folded side seams of piece A (fig. 50.13).

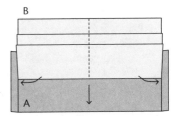

B

A

Fig. 50.13

14 Use the sewing machine to stitch along the sides and bottom to secure piece B to piece A (fig. 50.14). Then fold the wallet in half widthwise to finish.

Fig. 50.14

WHAT YOU NEED

- *Ruler*

- *Craft knife*

- *Self-healing cutting mat*

- *Scraps of papers in various colors and patterns (book pages and origami paper work well)*

- *Cylindrical objects of different widths for rolling: for example, toothpick, pencil, Sharpie, glue stick*

- *Small paintbrush*

- *Decoupage medium*

- *Acrylic sealer (optional)*

- *E6000 glue*

- *Pin back*

51 | Roll with It Brooch

LEVEL ● ● ● ○ ○

It's amazing how intricate this brooch looks when you consider that it's made of a few strips of tightly rolled paper and glue. That's pretty much all there is to it! The real fun is in the design—arranging the different sizes and colors of paper coils to create that perfect statement piece. It all comes together pretty organically, so just, you know, *roll* with it.

❶ Use the ruler, craft knife, and cutting mat to cut between eight and twelve strips of paper in various widths (³⁄₈" to ½") and lengths (4" to 10") (fig. 51.1).

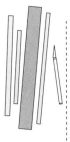

Fig. 51.1

❷ Select a paper strip and choose a cylindrical object to use as a rolling instrument. Starting at one end of the paper strip, roll the paper around the object once, then brush some decoupage medium on the next section of the strip and roll again. Continue rolling, adding decoupage medium after each rotation, until you reach the end of the paper strip. Add decoupage medium at the end of the strip to seal the coil (fig. 51.2).

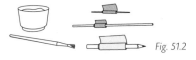

Fig. 51.2

❸ Repeat step 2 with the remaining strips and various rolling instruments, creating coils of different sizes (fig. 51.3).

Fig. 51.3

❹ Arrange the paper coils so that the denser ones (those with smaller holes) are in the center where the pin back will be attached. Brush decoupage medium on the sides of adjacent coils and hold them together until they bond (the medium won't be completely dry, but the coils will be stable enough to set down and attach more coils) (fig. 51.4). Let dry.

Fig. 51.4

❺ Brush a coat of decoupage medium over the coils to seal them. *Optional*: Or spray with a coat of acrylic sealer in a well-ventilated area. Let dry.

❻ Use the E6000 glue to attach the pin back to the flat side (the back) of the paper brooch (fig. 51.6). Let dry before wearing.

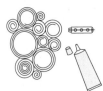

Fig. 51.6

52 | Off the Map Passport Cover

LEVEL ●●○○○

WHAT YOU NEED

. . . .

- Ruler
- Craft knife
- Self-healing cutting mat
- Map (at least 5½" by 11")
- Roll of clear contact paper
- Access to a sewing machine (with a leather or vinyl needle) and contrasting thread
- Scissors (for snipping thread)

A friend of mine was traveling back from Turkey recently and his passport was denied at customs because of a slightly torn page. I am a bit of a nervous flyer so you can imagine that this tale of woe sent shivers down my spine. I immediately designed a quick-and-easy but oh-so-cute passport cover for myself made, in subject-appropriate fashion, from maps.

❶ With a ruler, craft knife, and cutting mat, cut a 5¼" × 10¼" piece from your map. Cut two 5½" × 10½" pieces of contact paper.

❷ Peel the backing off one sheet of contact paper, center, and press it over the map.

❸ Peel the backing off the other sheet, center, and press it to the back of the map, sandwiching the map between the sheets (fig. 52.3). Press to seal, smoothing out any bubbles.

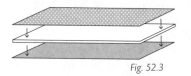

Fig. 52.3

❹ Lay the map assembly flat and fold each short side 1½" toward the center (fig. 52.4).

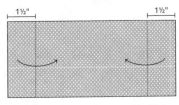

Fig. 52.4

❺ Use a straight stitch to sew around the perimeter of the passport cover (be sure to catch the folded layers in the seam) to create pockets (fig. 52.5). *Optional:* Stitch decorative lines over the map. Follow latitude and longitude lines, streets, or zigzag and swirl however you please.

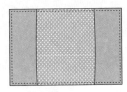

Fig. 52.5

❻ Insert the front and back covers of a passport into each of the pockets (fig. 52.6). Then fold it closed.

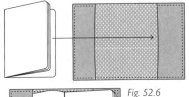

Fig. 52.6

53 | Lucky Star Cuff Links

LEVEL ⊗ ⊗ ⊗ ⊗ ⊗

Origami stars are absolutely addictive to make and, once you get the hang of them, a cinch, too. If you have a hard time thinking of good crafty gifts to give the special guy in your life, these origami star cuff links are pretty perfect.

WHAT YOU NEED

- 2 strips of regular-weight paper (½" × 11")
- Small paintbrush
- Decoupage medium
- Acrylic sealer (optional)
- E6000 glue
- A pair of cuff link blanks

1. Hold one strip of paper with the wrong side facing up and make a loop at one end, leaving a ½" tail overlapping the longer end (fig. 53.1).

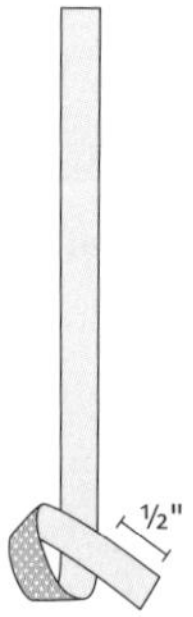

Fig. 53.1

2. Slip the long end through the loop and gently pull it tight to tie a knot. Then flatten the knot so that it forms a pentagon (fig. 53.2).

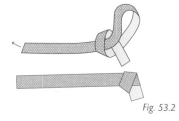

Fig. 53.2

3. Fold the short end and tuck it under a flap in the pentagon (fig. 53.3).

Fig. 53.3

4. Fold the long end of the strip diagonally over the pentagon, so the edge lines up with one side of the pentagon (fig. 53.4).

Fig. 53.4

5. Fold the long end of the strip diagonally over the pentagon again, lining up the edge with the side of the pentagon adjacent to the one in the previous fold (fig. 53.5).

Fig. 53.5

6. Repeat steps 4 and 5 (fig. 53.6) until the end of the strip is too short to fold again.

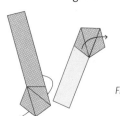

Fig. 53.6

7 Tuck the end under a flap in the pentagon as you did in step 3 (fig. 53.7).

  Fig. 53.7

8 Gently push the tip of your finger into each side of the pentagon to puff up the star (fig. 53.8).

  Fig. 53.8

9 Repeat steps 1 through 7 with the second strip of paper to make another star.

10 Use the brush to cover both stars with a thin layer of decoupage medium. Let dry and repeat two times to create a thick coat (fig. 53.10). *Optional:* Spray acrylic sealer on the front, back, and sides of the star and let dry.

Fig. 53.10

11 Apply a small dot of E6000 glue to the flat side of one cuff link blank and center it on a star. Repeat with the second blank and star to complete the pair of cuff links. Let dry.

VARIATION

Substitute earring blanks for the cuff links to make a pair of studs. String stars together to make a bracelet or a necklace. Or make a whole slew of stars for a decorative alternative to Styrofoam packing peanuts.

WHAT YOU NEED

- *Access to a computer with a printer and paper*
- *Petal, leaf, and fascinator templates**
- *Craft knife*
- *Self-healing cutting mat*
- *Pencil*
- *4 sheets "new paper" (8½" × 11" card stock or watercolor paper work well)*
- *Scissors*
- *White glue*
- *Small paintbrush*
- *Ruler*
- *1 sheet "old paper" (8½" × 11" lighter weight) or lots of smaller scraps*
- *Jewelry adhesive*
- *Haircomb*

54 | Something Old, Something New Fascinator

LEVEL ⊗ ⊗ ⊗ ⊗

I was not a traditional bride by any stretch of the imagination. But even though I didn't wear a big white dress or a veil, there were a few traditions that I couldn't part with. This paper flower fascinator is modern and unexpected, with healthy nods to the "Something Old, Something New" tradition in its use of new and old papers. My "old" papers came from an old family letter. (If you don't want to cut up a family heirloom, just scan and copy it.) Choose something that has a special meaning to you and your loved ones.

———— ◆ ————

1 Print the large and small petal templates and leaf templates and cut them out using the craft knife and cutting mat (fig. 54.1).

Fig. 54.1

2 Use the large template to trace and cut ten large flower petals from the "new" paper. Then use the small template to trace and cut five small flower petals, also from the "new" paper (fig. 54.2).

Fig. 54.2

3 Fold each of the fifteen petals in half and unfold (fig. 54.3).

Fig. 54.3

4 Separate the five large petals and cut a 1" slit at the point of each petal, along the fold line. Select the ten small petals, and cut a ½" slit at the point of each petal, along the fold line (fig. 54.4).

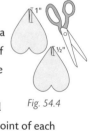

Fig. 54.4

5 Select one large petal. At the slit, overlap one edge of the paper on the other to create dimension in the petal. Glue along the edge. Repeat with each petal (fig. 54.5).

Fig. 54.5

* Download at workman.com/papermade

6 Select five large petals and glue
   them together in a circle, points
   in, overlapping them in the center
   (fig. 54.6). This creates one layer of
   the flower.

Fig. 54.6

7 Repeat step 6 with the remaining
   five large petals to make a second
   layer of the flower. Brush glue onto
   the bottom
   of the petals
   in this layer
   and insert it
   into the first
   (fig. 54.7).

Fig. 54.7

8 Repeat step 6 with the five small
   petals to make a third layer of the
   flower. Brush glue onto the bottom
   of the petals
   in this layer
   and insert
   it into the
   center of the
   second layer
   (fig. 54.8).

Fig. 54.8

9 Use the leaf template to trace and
   cut four leaves from the "new"
   paper (fig. 54.9).

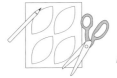

Fig. 54.9

⑩ Fold each of the four leaves in half and unfold (fig. 54.10).

Fig. 54.10

⑪ Use scissors to cut diagonal slits into the edges of each leaf to the center fold, creating fringe (this represents the veins on a leaf) (fig. 54.11).

Fig. 54.11

⑫ Arrange and glue the four leaves to the bottom of the flower (fig. 54.12).

Fig. 54.12

⑬ Measure and cut a 1" × 10" strip from the "old" paper and cut a fringe about halfway in along one long edge (fig. 54.13).

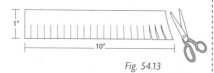

Fig. 54.13

⑭ Roll up the strip to make a 1" coil. Use the glue to secure the end of the roll (fig. 54.14).

Fig. 54.14

⑮ Measure and cut a 1" circle from the "old" paper. Fan out the fringe at the top of the roll from step 14, and center and glue the circle on the fanned-out fringe. The fringe should be visible around the edges of the circle (fig. 54.15).

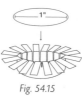

Fig. 54.15

⑯ Apply glue to the bottom of the paper coil and press it into the center of the flower (fig. 54.16).

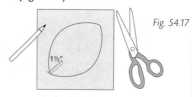

Fig. 54.16

⑰ Print the fascinator template onto white paper and cut it out. Trace the template onto the "new" paper and cut it out. Then mark and cut a 1½" slit into the edge, as shown (fig. 54.17).

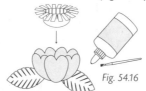

Fig. 54.17

⑱ At the slit, overlap one edge of the paper with the other to create dimension in the fascinator. Glue along the edge and trim the uneven edges (fig. 54.18).

Fig. 54.18

⑲ Draw and use scissors to cut about one hundred ½"-long teardrop shapes from the "old" paper (fig. 54.19).

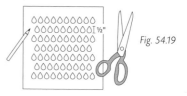

Fig. 54.19

⑳ Starting at the bottom of the fascinator (where the slit is), and overlapping the edges of the fascinator, glue on the teardrops in rows until the entire fascinator is covered (fig. 54.20).

Fig. 54.20

㉑ Use jewelry adhesive to glue the haircomb to the underside of the fascinator (fig. 54.21). Let dry.

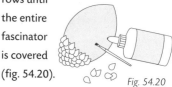

Fig. 54.21

㉒ Use jewelry adhesive to glue the flower to the top side of the fascinator base (fig. 54.22). Let dry.

Fig. 54.22

Spare a Square Desk
Organizer, page 159

Spare a Square Desk
Organizer, page 159

Signed, Sealed, Delivered
Accordion Book, page 170

Signed, Sealed, Delivered
Accordion Book, page 170

CHAPTER
. . . .
five

PAPER FOR
WRAPPING AND
WRITING

55 | Cup of Tea Cards

LEVEL ✪ ✪ ✪ ✪ ✪

It's so easy to keep in touch with friends now via e-mail and Facebook and text and instant messaging, but taking the time to write a little note to someone to let him or her know you really care is so, so much better. These cards are the perfect fit for a simple little note—it'll be like sharing a cup of tea with your best chum. I like to make a ton of them on a rainy afternoon and store them for all my correspondence needs.

WHAT YOU NEED

(makes 2 notecards)

- Access to a computer with a printer and paper
- Teacup templates*
- 1 sheet of card stock (8½" × 11")
- Bone folder
- Ruler
- Craft knife
- Self-healing cutting mat
- Pencil
- Decorative paper (scraps of wallpaper or wrapping paper work well)
- Glue stick
- Access to a sewing machine with contrasting thread (optional)

1. Print and cut out the teacup templates.

2. Fold the card stock in half widthwise and crease with a bone folder (fig. 55.2).

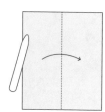

Fig. 55.2

3. Use the ruler, craft knife, and cutting mat to cut the folded piece of card stock in half, making two 4¼" × 5½" folded cards (fig. 55.3).

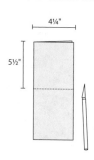

Fig. 55.3

4. Line up the handle of the teacup template along the folded edge of one card and trace. Cut out the traced shape through both layers of the card (fig. 55.4).

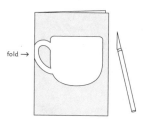

fold →

Fig. 55.4

5. Measure and cut decorative paper strips between ¼" × 10" and ¾" × 10" in size.

* Download at workman.com/papermade

6 Open the card and lay it flat, outsides facing up. Arrange the paper strips across the card and mark their locations with small pencil dots. Use a ruler to make sure the lines are straight. Apply an even coat of glue stick to the back of each strip and press it in place. Let dry, then trim the strips to fit the edges of the teacup (fig. 55.6a). *Optional:* Add some extra details to the card by stitching along the strips with a sewing machine—try using straight and zigzag stitches (fig. 55.6b). Trim the threads.

7 Once complete, refold the card.

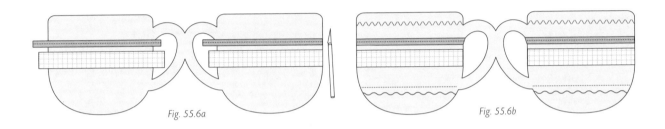

Fig. 55.6a   Fig. 55.6b

Season's Greetings

The custom of sending greeting cards, like many paper inventions, can be traced back to the ancient Chinese, who exchanged cards every New Year. The oldest valentine resides in the British Museum. But greeting cards really took off in the 1840s with the invention of . . . any guesses? The adhesive stamp!

WHAT YOU NEED

. . . .

- *Ruler*
- *Craft knife*
- *Self-healing cutting mat*
- *2 sheets of card stock (8½" × 11") in different colors*
- *Bone folder*
- *Access to a computer with a printer and paper*
- *Paris skyline templates**
- *Pencil*
- *Decorative paper scraps (book pages, maps, and wallpaper work well)*
- *Glue stick*
- *Typewriter or pen to write a greeting*
- *Decorative-edge scissors*

56 | *Bonne Chance Pop-Up Card*

LEVEL ✪✪✪✪✪

I have a friend who is really good at sending cards. For years, she lived right down the street from me, and still she would find the time to send a card just to wish me some good luck or encouragement. Here's your opportunity to help celebrate those tiny moments.

———◆———

1 Use the ruler, craft knife, and cutting mat to cut one 5½" × 8½" piece of card stock from each of the card stock sheets (fig 56.1).

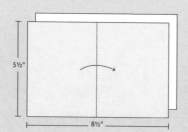

Fig. 56.1

2 Fold both pieces in half to make two 5½" × 4¼" cards. Crease the fold neatly with a bone folder (fig. 56.2).

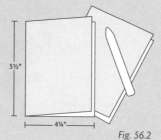

Fig. 56.2

3 Print and cut out the Paris skyline templates.

4 Trace the skyline templates onto different paper scraps and cut them out roughly. Set aside the Eiffel Tower and hot-air balloon pieces with some of the leftover card stock from step 1. Use glue stick to affix these pieces to the card stock and cut out with a craft knife. Lightly number the other buildings with a pencil so they correspond with the numbering on the templates.

5 Determine which color card stock from step 2 will be used for the inside of the card. Set aside the outside piece.

6 Fold the inside piece in half. Use a craft knife to cut three pairs of parallel lines through both layers,

* Download at workman.com/papermade

as depicted in fig. 56.6. The lines of each pair should be ¼" apart.

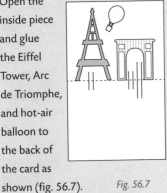

Fig. 56.6

7 Open the inside piece and glue the Eiffel Tower, Arc de Triomphe, and hot-air balloon to the back of the card as shown (fig. 56.7).

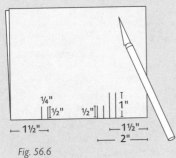

Fig. 56.7

8 Pop out the cuts that you made in step 6 (fig. 56.8a). Glue building 1 to the pop-ups created by the ½" cuts and glue building 2 to the pop-up created by the 1" cut (fig. 56.8b).

Fig. 56.8a

Fig. 56.8b

9 Cut a ¼" × 3" paper strip and fold it into a 1" × ½" rectangle. Glue the ends together (fig. 56.9).

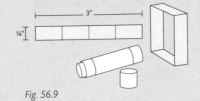

Fig. 56.9

10 Apply glue along just the 1" sides of the paper rectangle and attach the piece to the back of building 2 and the front of building 1 (fig. 56.10).

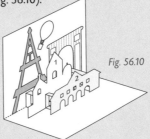

Fig. 56.10

11 Cut a ¼" × 3¼" paper strip and fold it into a 1" × ½" rectangle. Glue the ends together as you did in step 9 (fig. 56.11).

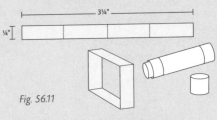

Fig. 56.11

12 Apply glue along just the ½" sides of the paper rectangle and attach the piece to the back of building 3 and the front of building 2 (fig. 56.12).

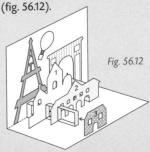

Fig. 56.12

13 Retrieve the outside of the card you cut and folded in steps 1 and 2. Lay it flat. Toward the bottom right of the card, trace a 2½"-diameter circle with a pencil and cut it out with a craft knife (fig. 56.13).

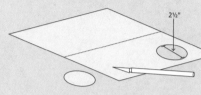

Fig. 56.13

14 Measure and cut a 3" square of paper. Apply glue around the inside edge of the circle and back it with the 3" square paper (fig. 56.14).

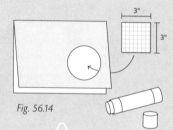

Fig. 56.14

15 Type or write out *"Bonne Chance!"* on another scrap of paper. Trace a circle around the message with the message centered. Cut around the circle with decorative-edge scissors. Coat the back with glue stick and attach it to the front of the card, centered on the circle (fig. 56.15).

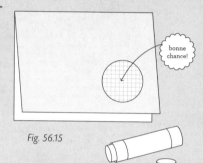

Fig. 56.15

16 Apply glue over the inside of the outer card. Slide the inside piece of the card into the outer piece and press the layers together (fig. 56.16). Let dry.

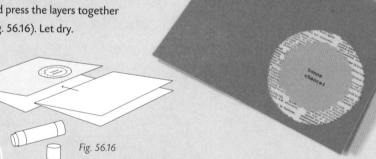

Fig. 56.16

Rags to Riches

Until the end of the 19th century, papermaking wasn't such an easy proposition: It involved large quantities of found and scavenged rags. This elaborate process must have been on the mind of the anonymous 18th-century English poet who penned the following verse:

RAGS make paper
PAPER makes money
MONEY makes banks
BANKS make loans
LOANS make beggars
BEGGARS make RAGS

57 | **Better Binder Clips**

LEVEL ✪ ✪ ✪ ✪ ✪

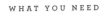

Boring office supplies begone! These aren't just your plain old run-of-the-mill binder clips; they're *better*. With any color or pattern combination you want, it's the ultimate marriage of form and function, don't you think?

———◆———

1 Fold one scrap of paper around the three metal sides of one binder clip and use the scissors to trim the edges if necessary.

2 Fold down the grips on the binder clip and brush decoupage medium on one side of the clip. Line up and press one edge of the paper to the side of the clip (fig. 57.2).

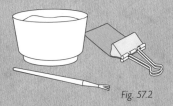

Fig. 57.2

3 Brush decoupage medium onto the other two sides of the clip and wrap and press the paper around the clip (fig. 57.3). Let dry for a few minutes.

Fig. 57.3

4 Brush decoupage medium over all three sides of the clip.

5 Repeat steps 1 through 4 to create more decorative clips. Let dry for a couple of hours.

WHAT YOU NEED
....

- 1½" × ¾" lightweight *paper scraps*
- *Small (¾") binder clips*
- *Small scissors*
- *Small paintbrush*
- *Decoupage medium*

58 | **Pleased and Punched Cards**

LEVEL ⊗ ⊗ ⊗ ⊗ ⊗

WHAT YOU NEED
. . . .

(makes 2 note cards)

- *2 sheets of card stock (8½" × 11") in green and blue*
- *Bone folder*
- *Ruler*
- *Craft knife*
- *Self-healing cutting mat*
- *Access to a computer with a printer and paper*
- *Toadstool templates**
- *Tracing paper*
- *Pencil*
- *¼" circle hole punch*
- *Paper scraps: red, white, brown, yellow, light green, dark green*
- *Small paintbrush*
- *White glue*
- *Glue stick*

Talk about a way to use up your paper scraps! You can make these punched paper cards out of the tiniest bits of paper. Junk mail, magazines, wrapping paper, old cards, and even paint chips are the perfect colorful raw materials for paper punching. This is also a great project for the whole family—there's no pressure to make perfectly straight marks or color in the lines. Pass a bowlful of paper dots, some nontoxic glue, and a sheet of card stock and everybody can go to town!

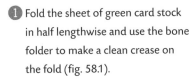

1 Fold the sheet of green card stock in half lengthwise and use the bone folder to make a clean crease on the fold (fig. 58.1).

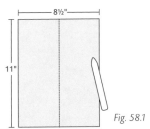

Fig. 58.1

2 Use the ruler, craft knife, and cutting mat to cut the folded piece of card stock in half to make two 4¼" × 5½" cards (fig. 58.2).

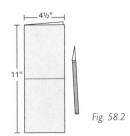

Fig. 58.2

3 Cut two 3¾" × 5" rectangles from the blue card stock (fig. 58.3). Set them aside.

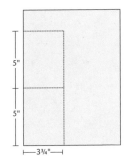

Fig. 58.3

4 Print the toadstool templates. Layer a piece of tracing paper over the templates and trace them (fig. 58.4).

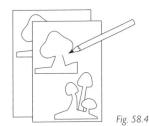

Fig. 58.4

* Download at workman.com/papermade

5 Flip the sheet of tracing paper over, center one of the toadstools over a piece of blue card stock, and trace over the toadstools again. This will transfer a light pencil outline onto the card (fig. 58.5). Using the same technique, trace the second toadstool onto the remaining piece of blue card stock.

Fig. 58.5

6 Use the hole punch to punch dozens of dots from each color of scrap paper. Sort them into piles by color.

7 Brush a tiny bit of glue on the back of a white dot and place it in a toadstool outline where the stem would be. Continue filling in the stem(s) with white dots. Use red or yellow dots for the top of the toadstools, white or brown dots for the spots, and light and dark green dots for the ground. Erase your pencil lines as you work (fig. 58.7).

Fig. 58.7

8 When the toadstool outlines are filled with paper dots, let the pieces of blue card stock dry for one hour.

9 Spread the glue stick across the back of one piece of blue card stock and center it on the front of one of the folded green cards. Repeat with the second piece of card stock and remaining green cards (fig. 58.9). *Note:* Before you press to stick them on, make sure your card is right side up and opens on the right.

Fig. 58.9

59 | Gift Wrapping Is in the (Paper Lunch) Bags

LEVEL ● ● ○ ○ ○

WHAT YOU NEED

....

(makes 4 different bags)

- *Paper lunch bags*
- *Zigzag-edge scissors*
- *¼" circle hole punch*
- *Baker's twine*
- *Scraps of colored paper, newspaper, and tissue paper*
- *Pencil*
- *Ruler*
- *Scissors*
- *Craft knife*
- *Self-healing cutting mat*
- *Glue stick*

Picture this: It's seven thirty, you just got home from work and barely have time to change and eat something before a birthday party at eight. Keys in hand, you're just about to run out the door when you realize: "Oh, no, I forgot to wrap the present! And come to think of it, I don't even have gift wrap!" Relax. You can still creatively wrap up your present in a few minutes. Here are four different methods, using little more than a paper lunch bag.

The Laced-Up Bag

1. With the bag flattened, use the zigzag-edge scissors to cut about 1" off the top of the bag. Then punch six holes about 1" apart along both sides of the bag. Make sure to punch through all the layers of the bag (fig. 59.1.1).

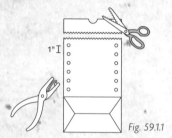

Fig. 59.1.1

2. Cut a 3' length of twine. Open the bag and tie one end in a knot at the front bottom right hole (hole 1A). Thread the twine across the front of the bag and through hole 2B (opposite and above hole 1A), then around the side of the bag and through hole 2C on the back (fig. 59.1.2).

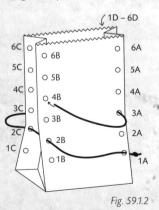

Fig. 59.1.2

3. Thread the twine through hole 3D on the back, and then around the side of the bag and through hole 3A. Continue in this manner until you reach the top of the bag (hole 6B). Then thread the twine back down around the bag, through the unused holes and crossing the twine already in place (fig. 59.1.3).

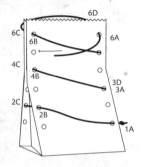

Fig. 59.1.3

4. Tie the end of the twine to the back of the bag, opposite the first knot, at hole 1D (fig. 59.1.4).

Fig. 59.1.4

5. Cut a 3" square from colored paper with the zigzag-edge scissors and then cut a 2½" square from another paper bag. Glue the smaller square, centered, on the larger square to use as a gift tag (fig. 59.1.5).

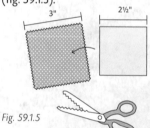

Fig. 59.1.5

6. Punch a hole, centered, along one side of the tag, ½" in from the edge. Thread a short length of twine through the hole, then through a hole at the top of the bag, and tie the ends together (fig. 59.1.6).

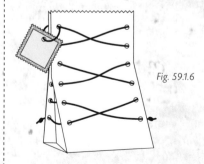

Fig. 59.1.6

The Paper Cuts Bag

1 Use the zigzag-edge scissors to cut about 2" off the top of the bag and set aside the excess (fig. 59.2.1).

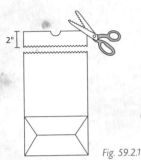

2"

2 Fold the bag in half lengthwise and then in half again, making a long strip (fig. 59.2.2).

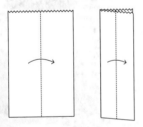

Fig. 59.2.2

3 Use regular scissors to cut shapes into the folds, as if you were making a paper snowflake (fig. 59.2.3). Unfold the bag, open it up, and set it aside.

Fig. 59.2.3

4 Cut a 2" square of newspaper with the zigzag-edge scissors. Cut a 1½" piece from the top of the paper bag that you cut off in step 1. Center and glue the paper bag square onto the newspaper square to create a gift tag (fig. 59.2.4).

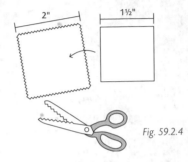

2"   1½"

Fig. 59.2.4

5 Punch a hole, centered, along one side of the tag, ½" in from the edge. Thread a short length of twine through the hole, then through a hole at the top of the bag, and tie the ends together.

6 Stuff the bag with brightly colored tissue paper (fig. 59.2.6).

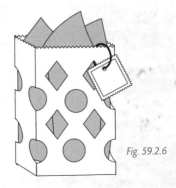

Fig. 59.2.6

The Buttoned-Up Bag

① Trace a 4"-diameter circle on a sheet of newspaper and cut it out using the zigzag-edge scissors. Cut a 3½"-diameter circle from the colored paper. Center and glue the colored circle onto the newspaper circle to create a gift tag (fig. 59.3.1).

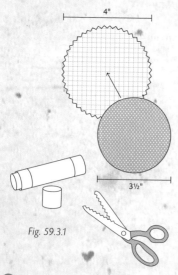

Fig. 59.3.1

② Punch a hole along the side of the tag, about ½" from the edge. Punch a second hole opposite the first (fig. 59.3.2).

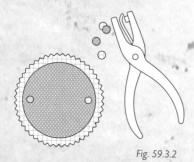

Fig. 59.3.2

③ Fold the top of the bag down twice, about 1½" (fig. 59.3.3).

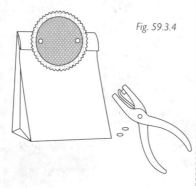

Fig. 59.3.3

④ Center the tag along the front of the fold. Punch two holes through the fold, lining them up with the holes in the tag (fig. 59.3.4).

Fig. 59.3.4

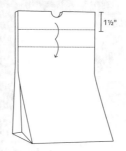

⑤ Thread a short length of twine through each of the holes in the bag fold and then through the holes in the tag (fig. 59.3.5a). Tie the ends in a bow in the center of the tag (fig. 59.3.5b).

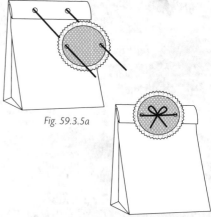

Fig. 59.3.5a

Fig. 59.3.5b

The Woven-Handle Bag

1 Use the zigzag-edge scissors to cut about 1" off the top of the bag. Then use the ruler, craft knife, and cutting mat to cut five centered 1" horizontal slits down the length of the bag through both layers (fig. 59.4.1).

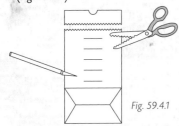

Fig. 59.4.1

2 Measure and cut a ⅞" × 22" strip of newspaper and a ¾" × 23" strip of colored paper.

3 Center and glue the colored paper over the newspaper so that a little bit of the colored paper hangs off the newspaper on both ends. Cut a V shape into the end of the colored paper strip (fig. 59.4.3).

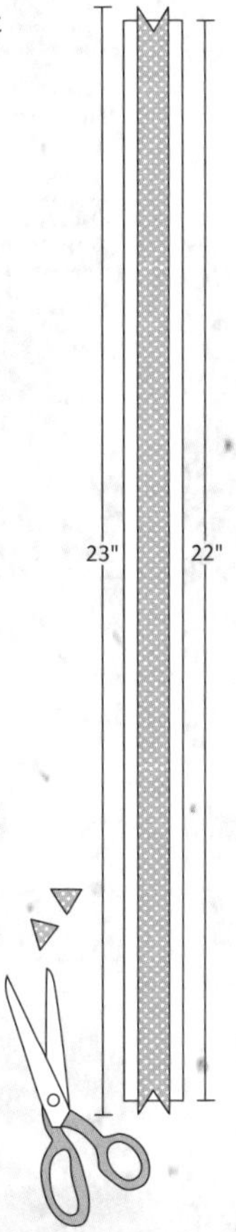

23"   22"

Fig. 59.4.3

4 To turn the strip into a handle, weave one end of the paper strip, from the inside to the outside, through each of the top slits in the paper bag. Then thread the ends from outside to inside, through the next slits on either side of the bag. Continue down the bag until the ends of the strip appear through the bottom slits on the outside of the bag. Glue the inside end of each strip to the outside of the bag to secure it (fig. 59.4.4).

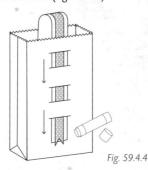

Fig. 59.4.4

5 Trace a 2"-diameter circle on a sheet of colored paper and cut it out using the zigzag-edge scissors to make a gift tag (fig. 59.4.5). Punch a hole at the side of the tag, ½" from the edge.

2"

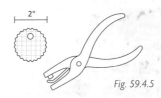

Fig. 59.4.5

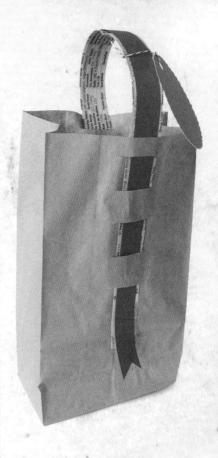

6 Thread a small length of twine through the hole in the tag and around the handle of the bag, and tie the ends together (fig. 59.4.6).

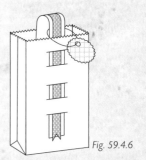

Fig. 59.4.6

60 | I Dig You Card

LEVEL ⓧⓧⓧⓧⓧ

What to do when you want to say "I love you," but you just can't bear to send another cheeseball, syrupy-sweet card from the stationery store? Before you submit yourself or your loved one to those well-rehearsed sentimental platitudes, grab some paper and scissors and try this silly but heartfelt pun on for size.

WHAT YOU NEED

- *Ruler*
- *Craft knife*
- *Self-healing cutting mat*
- *2 sheets of colored paper (8½" × 11") in different shades*
- *Bone folder*
- *Access to a computer with a printer and paper*
- *Words and veggies templates**
- *Pencil*
- *Small scraps of paper (at least 4" × 4") in various colors*
- *Glue stick*

1 Use the ruler, craft knife, and cutting mat to cut a 10" × 5" rectangle from each sheet of paper. Set aside the excess paper.

2 Fold each rectangle in half to make a square, and crease the folds neatly with the bone folder (fig. 60.2).

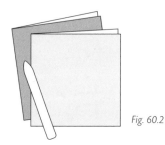

Fig. 60.2

3 Print and cut out the words and veggies templates (fig. 60.3).

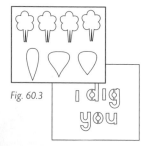

Fig. 60.3

4 Trace three veggies and four greens templates onto scraps of paper. Cut out the shapes and apply glue stick to the top back of each veggie to attach the greens (two greens for each veggie) (fig. 60.4).

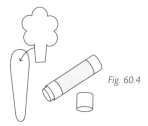

Fig. 60.4

5 From the paper left over in step 1, cut three ¼" × 3" strips. Glue each one vertically along the back of each of the veggies to make them more stable (fig. 60.5).

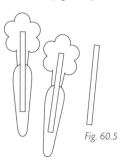

Fig. 60.5

* Download at workman.com/papermade

6 Select one of the folded pieces from step 1 to be the outside of the card. Unfold it and lay it flat. Layer the words template over the front outside of the card and trace with a pencil (fig. 60.6).

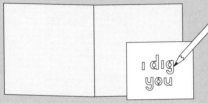

Fig. 60.6

7 Use the craft knife to carefully cut out the words.

8 Use the ruler and pencil to mark a horizontal line along the center of the front of the card. Cut three slits about 1¼" wide and ¼" apart along the line in the card (fig. 60.8). (These are pockets for the veggies.)

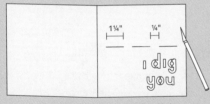

Fig. 60.8

9 Flip the card over and line the perimeter of the card with glue stick. Press the remaining folded piece from step 1 inside the outer card and press together along the edges (fig. 60.9). Let dry.

Fig. 60.9

10 Refold the card and tuck the veggies into the slits on the front (fig. 60.10).

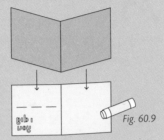

Fig. 60.10

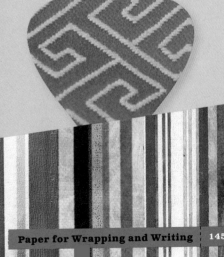

WHAT YOU NEED

- Access to a computer with a printer and paper
- Out to sea card templates 1–3*
- Pencil
- Tracing paper
- Sheet of card stock (15" × 7")
- Bone folder
- Craft knife
- Self-healing cutting mat
- Ruler
- Map scrap (5" × 7")
- Glue stick
- Tiny paper scrap (at least 2" × 2") for the fish

61 | Out to Sea Card

LEVEL ⊗ ⊗ ⊗ ⊘ ⊘

Ahoy! Concertina cards are my favorite kind of cards because, with a few cuts and folds, you can turn something flat into something beautifully dimensional. Landscapes are the best subjects for this type of card because you can really capture the foreground and background of a scene, from the little fish swimming way down deep, to the whale's tail just visible over the waves, to a tugboat floating along in the distance.

---

1 Print the out to sea card templates and trace them with a pencil onto tracing paper. Then set them aside.

2 Fold the card stock in half and crease with the bone folder (fig. 61.2). Unfold.

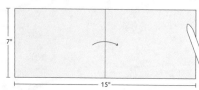

Fig. 61.2

3 Fold the front of the card to meet the spine. Repeat with the back of the card to create an accordion fold. Crease with the bone folder (fig. 61.3).

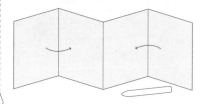

Fig. 61.3

4 Orient the paper so that the top fold of the paper is on the right, the middle (original) fold is on the left, and the bottom fold is on the right. In the corner of each panel, lightly mark the numbers 1 through 4 (fig. 61.4).

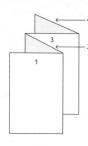

Fig. 61.4

* Download at workman.com/papermade

5 Open the card. Lay the traced template 1 on panel 1, right sides facing, and trace carefully over the pencil lines to transfer your design. Repeat, pairing and tracing the templates on panels 2 and 3 (fig. 61.5).

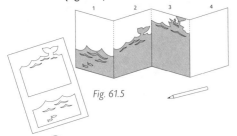

Fig. 61.5

6 Use the craft knife and cutting mat to carefully cut along the marked lines on panels 1 through 3 (fig. 61.6). Gently erase all stray pencil marks.

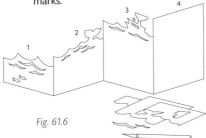

Fig. 61.6

7 Measure and cut a 5" x 7" rectangle from the map. Cover the back of the map with the glue stick and press it onto the front of panel 4 (fig. 61.7).

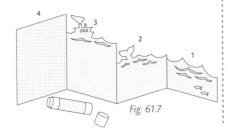

Fig. 61.7

8 Trace and cut out two fish from the tiny scrap papers. Use the glue stick to attach them to the front of panel 1 (fig. 61.8).

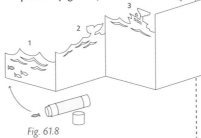

Fig. 61.8

9 Fold up the card and you're ready to gift it (fig. 61.9).

Fig. 61.9

WHAT YOU NEED

- *Access to a computer with a printer and paper*
- *Petal envelope and cupcake templates**
- *Pencil*
- *Paper for the CD envelope (kraft paper works well)*
- *Craft knife*
- *Self-healing cutting mat*
- *Glue stick*
- *Paper for the lining (graph paper works well)*
- *Scissors*
- *Ruler*
- *Bone folder*
- *Tissue paper or other colored paper in a variety of shades*
- *½" circle hole punch*
- *Typewriter or pen*
- *Sewing machine (optional)*
- *Paper for the track listing insert (colored paper works well)*
- *CD*
- *A sticker*

62 | Birthday Cake Mix

LEVEL ●●●○○

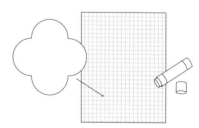

The handcrafted mixtape was a very important part of my adolescence: I would pore over song lyrics to make sure I was sending would-be boyfriends the right messages, find obscure B-sides to impress my music nerd friends, and obsess over the perfect cover art collage. Music has the power to make a big statement; anyone who has ever seen the movie *High Fidelity* knows what I'm talking about. These days, mixtapes are obsolete. Heck, even CDs seem quaintly retro. All the more reason to make a birthday mix CD before the art is entirely lost.

---

1 Print the petal envelope template and the cupcake template and cut them out.

2 Trace the petal envelope template onto the kraft paper to make half the envelope. Flip the template over and trace it to complete the envelope. Use the craft knife and cutting mat to cut it out (fig. 62.2).

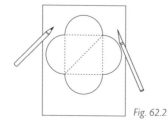

Fig. 62.2

3 Spread the glue stick over the inside of the kraft paper envelope and press it onto the graph paper. Use the craft knife to trim off the excess graph paper around the edges (fig. 62.3).

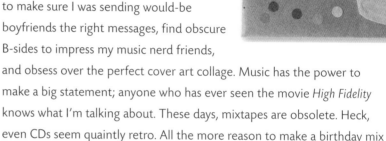

Fig. 62.3

* Download at workman.com/papermade

4 Use the ruler and the pencil to lightly draw in the fold lines for the envelope. Then use the bone folder to crease at the fold lines (fig. 62.4). Unfold and erase the pencil marks.

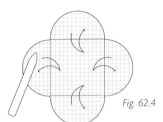

Fig. 62.4

5 Trace each piece of the cupcake template onto the desired tissue paper color and cut it out with scissors. Use the hole punch to create confetti dots in a few different colors (fig. 62.5).

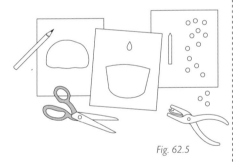

Fig. 62.5

6 Arrange and glue the cupcake pieces and confetti (as sprinkles) to the outside (front) of the envelope (fig. 62.6).

Fig. 62.6

7 Type or handwrite the name of the music mix onto the graph paper and cut it out with the craft knife. Then glue it to the front of the envelope (fig. 62.7). *Optional:* Use a sewing machine to stitch a few decorative details.

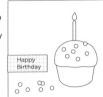

Happy Birthday

Fig. 62.7

8 Measure and cut a 4" square of colored paper with the craft knife. Then type or handwrite the CD track list onto the square, using both sides if necessary.

9 Orient the envelope so that the front is facing down, and place the CD and track listing inside (fig. 62.9). *Optional:* Make more tissue paper confetti and sprinkle it in the envelope.

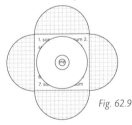

Fig. 62.9

10 Fold in each of the petals of the envelope one at a time to close, and seal with a sticker (fig. **62.10**).

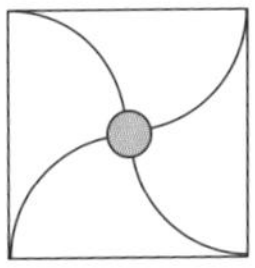

Fig. 62.10

❖

Pop Secret

Early pop-up books were definitely not made for children! "Movable books" were in use as early as the 14th century. They were mostly used to teach anatomy. Separate leaves, each featuring a different section of the body, could be hinged together at the top and attached to a page. This technique enabled the viewer to unfold, for instance, multiple depths of a torso, from rib cage to abdomen to spine.

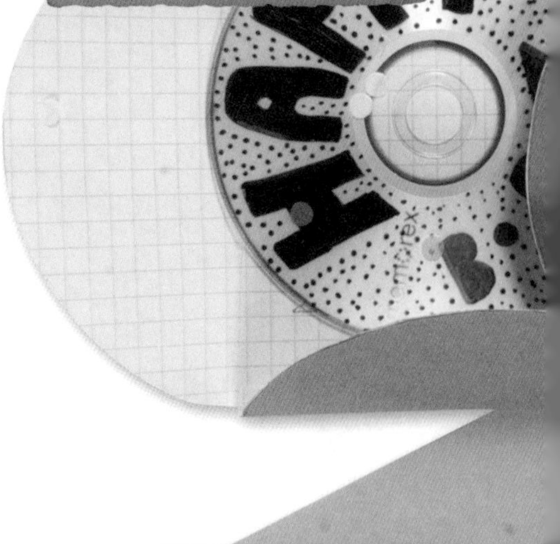

Money-Makin' Origami Heart

WHAT YOU NEED

- 1 crisp paper bill (the denomination is up to you!)
- 3½" × 9" piece of wax paper
- Access to a sewing machine and thread in desired color
- Zigzag-edge scissors

It's true that money can't buy you love, but sometimes, if you learn a few simple steps, it can make you hearts. There are some occasions in life when a cash gift seems most appropriate: a wedding, a graduation, your niece's thirteenth birthday. It's not the most creative gift on earth, but that's when the presentation can be fun! A crisp folded heart tucked into a wax paper sleeve is the perfect way to give some cash, DIY-style.

1 Fold the paper bill in half lengthwise, crease, and unfold (fig. 63.1).

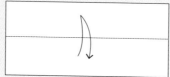

Fig. 63.1

2 Fold the bill in half widthwise, crease, and unfold (fig. 63.2).

Fig. 63.2

3 Fold up the bottom edge of the bill lengthwise to meet the horizontal center fold (fig. 63.3).

Fig. 63.3

4 Fold the lower right corner up diagonally to meet the vertical center fold as shown (fig. 63.4). Repeat for the left corner.

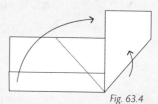

Fig. 63.4

5 Flip the bill over. Fold in the right edge to meet the nearest vertical fold. Repeat for the left edge (fig. 63.5).

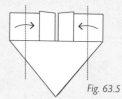

Fig. 63.5

6 Fold down the top flaps to meet the horizontal fold (fig. 63.6).

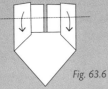

Fig. 63.6

7 Fold in the left and right corners diagonally, about ⅜", on both sides to complete the heart (fig. 63.7). Set it aside.

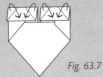

Fig. 63.7

8 Fold the sheet of wax paper in half and crease.

9 Use the sewing machine to stitch ¼" in along both long sides and the folded short side, backstitching at the beginning and the end (fig. 63.9).

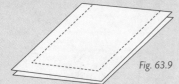

Fig. 63.9

10 Use the zigzag-edge scissors to trim all four sides of the sleeve before tucking the heart inside (fig. 63.10).

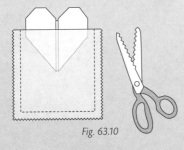

Fig. 63.10

The Color of Money

Paper artist Justine Smith's (justinesmith .net) favorite material is paper money from around the world. Her sculptures include an exquisite orchid crafted from *manat* (Turkmenistan's colorful currency) a pistol sculpted from one-dollar bills, and a stately pup made with UK pounds— each an artistic and social commentary on society's relationship with money.

64 | Paper Pillow Boxes

LEVEL ⊗ ⊗ ⊗ ⊗ ⊗

Why buy expensive gift boxes when you can make them yourself? These little pillow boxes are deceptively easy to construct and are a perfect container for small gifts (see the Lucky Star Cuff Links, page 124, or the Blooms and Berries Barrettes, page 108, for small gift ideas!). For interesting cardboard food packaging sources, check out foreign supermarkets or specialty food shops. I made these samples out of tea and cookie boxes from the Asian grocery in my neighborhood—of course I enjoyed the tea and cookies first!

WHAT YOU NEED

(makes 2 boxes)

- *Access to a computer with a printer and paper*
- *Pillow box template**
- *Lightweight cardboard from food packaging (cracker or cereal boxes work well)*
- *Pencil*
- *Glue stick*
- *Ruler*
- *Craft knife*
- *Self-healing cutting mat*
- *Hot glue gun and glue*
- *1 yard string or twine (optional)*

1 Print the pillow box template and cut it out using a craft knife and cutting mat. Open up and flatten the lightweight cardboard

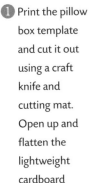
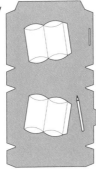

Fig. 64.1

packaging, wrong side up. Trace the template onto the large panels of cardboard (fig. 64.1). *Note:* Tracing onto the largest panels helps to avoid the seams in the packaging.

2 Cut around the tracings and transfer the dashed lines from the template. Lightly score the dashed lines on the cardboard (fig. 64.2).

Fig. 64.2

3 Fold both cardboard pieces in half at one score line and then fold over the flaps at the second score line.

4 Squeeze a line of hot glue along the inside edge of each of the flaps and press it to the outside of the opposite edge to create a somewhat cylindrical shape (fig. 64.4).

Fig. 64.4

5 Gently fold in both end flaps on either side of the boxes (fig. 64.5). *Optional:* Wrap the boxes with string or twine.

Fig. 64.5

* Download at workman.com/papermade

WHAT YOU NEED

- *Foam brush*
- *White glue*
- *Card stock (manila folders work well)*
- *Newspaper page (or other decorative paper)*
- *Access to a computer with a printer and paper*
- *Roof and house templates**
- *Ruler*
- *Craft knife*
- *Self-healing cutting mat*
- *Pencil*
- *Hot glue gun and glue*
- *Yarn or ribbon (approximately ¼ yard)*

65 | Home Sweet Gift Box

LEVEL ✪✪✪✪✪

What better way to give a housewarming gift than with a house-shaped gift box? This mini-house gift box is the perfect abode for a gift card, check, a set of coasters, a spare key, or any small token. I used the real estate pages from my Sunday newspaper, but you can shingle your house with any decorative paper.

❶ Brush glue over one side of the cardboard and press it down onto the newspaper. Let dry.

❷ Print the roof and house templates and cut them out using a ruler, craft knife, and cutting mat (fig. 65.2).

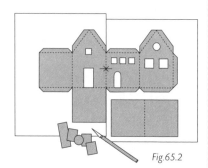

Fig. 65.2

❸ Line up the templates on the back of the card stock, tape them down, and use a pencil to trace them. Draw in the fold lines as indicated on the templates.

❹ Use the craft knife to cut along the traced lines. Be particularly careful cutting away the doors and windows. Score the fold lines.

❺ Fold and assemble the base of the house using hot glue to secure the pieces (fig. 65.5).

Fig. 65.5

❻ Add the roof to the top of the box and tie a ribbon or piece of yarn around the base and roof as shown (fig. 65.6).

Fig. 65.6

* Download at workman.com/papermade

❖

A Newsworthy House

The Paper House in Rockport, Massachusetts, didn't get its name for nothing. While the frame of the house is made from wood, the insulation and outside of the home is made from layers and layers of newspaper glued together and varnished on the outside to make it waterproof. So far so good. Though it requires yearly revarnishing, the house has been standing since 1924!

WHAT YOU NEED

. . . .

- Access to a computer with a printer and paper
- Gift bag templates*
- Craft knife
- Self-healing cutting mat
- Paper shopping bag
- Ruler
- Pencil
- Painter's tape
- Bone folder
- White glue
- 1' leather cord

66 | Big Bag, Little Bag Gift Bag

LEVEL ✪ ✪ ✪ ✪ ✪

Even the most vigilant among us forget to bring our cloth bags to the supermarket from time to time and have to ask for paper. Instead of throwing the bags in the recycling bin as soon as you've loaded up the fridge, save a few and transform them into mini woven gift bags. If you don't have leather cord for the bag handles, try yarn, ribbon, or twine.

———◆———

1 Print the gift bag templates and cut them out using a craft knife and cutting mat.

2 From the paper bag, cut thirty ½"× 9" strips and twenty ½" × 14" strips.

3 Lay out all of the ½" × 14" strips horizontally. On one side of the paper, press a strip of tape perpendicular along the edges, temporarily attaching the strips to your work surface (fig. 66.3).

Fig. 66.3

4 Weave the first ½" × 9" strip vertically through the horizontal strips, working it over and under, over and under (fig. 66.4). Slide the strip so it aligns with the taped edge.

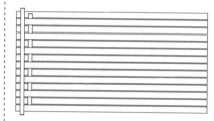

Fig. 66.4

5 Weave the second ½" × 9" strip through the horizontal strips, this time working it under and over, under and over. Then slide the strip over so it aligns with the first strip. Repeat with the remaining vertical strips, alternating over-under and under-over to create the woven pattern.

* Download at workman.com/papermade

6 Center the template over the woven strips, tape it in place, and cut away the excess (fig. 66.6).

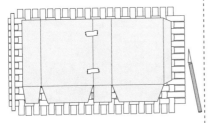

Fig. 66.6

7 With the template still taped to the woven panel, fold along the dotted lines of the template. Crease with a bone folder, then carefully remove the template (fig. 66.7).

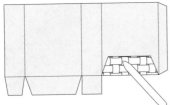

Fig. 66.7

8 Apply a dot of white glue to the ends of each strip along each side of the panel and press them to the overlapping pieces to secure the weaving.

9 Assemble the bag according to the template, and glue the bottom flaps and side overlaps together (fig. 66.9). Let dry.

Fig. 66.9

10 Cut the leather cord in half to make two 6" pieces. Select one piece and make a double overhand knot at one end.

11 Thread the unknotted end of the cord from the inside front of the bag, about 2" from one side of the bag, to the outside (fig. 66.11). Then reinsert the cord 2" from the other side of the bag, double knotting it on the inside of the bag.

Fig. 66.11

12 Repeat steps 10 and 11 on the back of the bag with the second piece of cord.

Off-the-Wall Paper

In response to the many tons of newspapers tossed away every day, designer Lori Weitzner found a solution to the problem: a new "wallpaper" called *Newsworthy* made from strips of newspaper on a hand loom!

(makes 1 set of pencils)

- Tape measure or ruler
- Unsharpened colored or plain pencil set (make sure the pencils are round and not hexagonal)
- Craft knife
- Self-healing cutting mat
- Scraps of paper that are at least as long as the pencils and 1" wide
- Foam brush
- Decoupage medium

67 | All Covered Up Pencils

LEVEL ✖ ✖ ✖ ✖ ✖

Office supplies are pretty standard-issue—black stapler, yellow pencils, metal binder clips—but they certainly don't have to be. This incredibly simple project transforms any plain pencil into something really special. Paper-covered pencils are a perfect gift for a writer or artist. I covered these samples with paper colors that correspond to the pencil color, but you can make a set of pencils to match a pencil cup on your desk, a notebook or sketch-pad cover, or each other—any lost pencil will be easily matched to its mates, and its owner!

1. Measure the length of the pencils. Use the tape measure or ruler, craft knife, and cutting mat to cut paper rectangles that are 1" wide by the length of your pencil (fig. 67.1). *Note:* If your pencil has an eraser, measure from the unsharpened end to the beginning of the metal eraser piece.

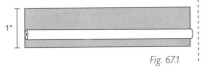

1"

Fig. 67.1

2. Lay flat one paper rectangle, wrong side up, and apply a layer of decoupage medium to the surface. Place the pencil about ¼" in from one long edge of the paper, lining up the ends of the pencil with the short ends of the rectangle (fig. 67.2).

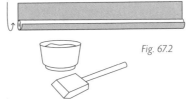

Fig. 67.2

3. Roll the long edge of the paper to meet the side of the pencil and slowly roll the pencil until it's covered (fig. 67.3).

Fig. 67.3

4. Spread a small amount of decoupage medium to the seam of the paper to seal it. Check your work to smooth out any creases or bubbles.

5. Repeat steps 2 through 4 to cover the remaining pencils. Let dry for one hour before sharpening (fig. 67.5).

Fig. 67.5

68 | Spare a Square Desk Organizer

LEVEL ✪ ✪ ✪ ✪ ✪

Who could forget that episode of *Seinfeld:* Elaine finds herself in a TP-free bathroom stall, and the woman in the stall next door refuses to help her out, insisting that she has not a "square to spare." Unlike that little square of toilet paper Elaine so desperately needed, the toilet paper tube itself doesn't have much inherent value; it's something we regularly toss out with little thought. But all that TP tube needs is a little TLC. A few pretty papers and a ribbon can completely transform tubes destined for the recycling bin into very useful office organizers.

- *Tape measure or ruler*
- *4 toilet paper tubes of equal size*
- *Craft knife*
- *Self-healing cutting mat*
- *3 sheets of lightweight paper (8½" × 11")*
- *Foam brush*
- *Decoupage medium*
- *Scissors*
- *Pencil*
- *5" square noncorrugated cardboard (food packaging works well)*
- *½ yard ribbon*
- *Hot glue gun and glue*

1. Use the tape measure or ruler to measure the circumference of one toilet paper tube and add ½" to get x. Then measure the length of the tube and add 2" to get y. Use the craft knife and cutting mat to cut four $x" \times y"$ pieces of paper.

2. Brush one tube with decoupage medium, center it along one edge of one sheet of paper, and roll the paper around it (fig. 68.2). Repeat for the remaining three tubes.

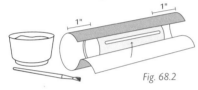
Fig. 68.2

3. Use scissors to cut 1" slits ¼" apart into the paper that extends on both sides of the tubes to create fringe (fig. 68.3).

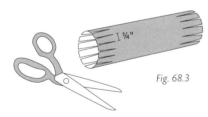
Fig. 68.3

4. Brush the inside of the fringe with decoupage medium and carefully press it to the inside of the tube. Repeat for the remaining three tubes (fig. 68.4).

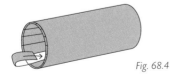
Fig. 68.4

5. Cut four pieces of $x"$ by (y – 2½") paper. (The sheets should be the same width as the sheets cut in step 1 but ½" shorter than the length of the toilet paper tube.)

6. Roll one sheet of paper so the right side is facing in, and brush the outside with decoupage medium. Insert the rolled paper inside the toilet paper tube (fig. 68.6). Center the paper ¼" in from the edges of the tube at both ends and unroll slowly so that the remaining paper lies smoothly against the inside of the toilet paper tube. Repeat for the remaining three tubes.

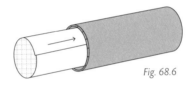
Fig. 68.6

7. Brush decoupage medium along the outside seam of each of the tubes. Cluster the tubes together, two by two, and apply more decoupage medium as needed to glue them together. Let dry (fig. 68.7).

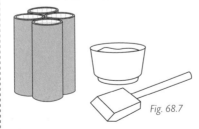
Fig. 68.7

8. Use the pencil to trace around the bottom of the cluster of tubes on noncorrugated cardboard. Cut out the shape with a craft knife to create the base (fig. 68.8).

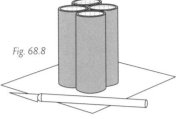
Fig. 68.8

9. Brush the bottoms of the tubes with decoupage medium and glue them to the base (fig. 68.9). Let dry.

Fig. 68.9

10. Brush decoupage medium over the entire outside and a few inches into the insides of the tubes and let dry. Repeat.

11. Measure the height of the toilet paper rolls and use the pencil to lightly mark the center point on one. Wrap the ribbon, level with the mark, around all four rolls and hot glue it in place. Trim the ends of the ribbon so they overlap about ½". Fold the end of the overlapping ribbon under for a clean finish and glue it in place (fig. 68.11).

Fig. 68.11

- *Lightweight cardboard from food packaging (cracker or cereal boxes work well)*
- *Self-healing cutting mat*
- *Ruler*
- *Craft knife*
- *Foam brush*
- *White glue*
- *1 piece of decorative paper about the size of one wide side of the cardboard box*
- *12 sheets of recycled office, notebook, or scrap paper*
- *Pencil*
- *4 binder clips*
- *Access to a sewing machine with vinyl or leather sewing needle and standard thread*

69 The Amazing 10-Minute Notebook

LEVEL ✪ ✪ ✪ ✪ ✪

I am a little bit of a notebook junkie—I keep a few at work for projects, inspiration, and to-do lists; a stack at home for writing, sketching, and more to-do lists; and one in my purse. With all the notebooks I go through, it was time to stop buying and start making. Why buy, after all, when you can DIY? Here's a notebook that won't squeeze your wallet or your schedule.

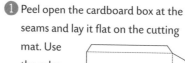

1 Peel open the cardboard box at the seams and lay it flat on the cutting mat. Use the ruler and a craft knife to carefully cut out the front panel and top flap of the box (fig. 69.1).

Fig. 69.1

2 Brush an even coat of glue over the front of the box and cover it with the sheet of decorative paper. Trim the excess from around the edges.

3 Measure the width and length of the front panel not including the tab flap (fig. 69.3).

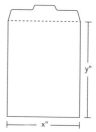

Fig. 69.3

4 Stack twelve sheets of paper (for the pages) and use the ruler and a pencil to measure and mark a rectangle on the top sheet that is ¼" smaller in width and length than the cardboard panel (fig. 69.4).

5 Line up the sheets and clamp them together with the binder clips to keep them from shifting. Use the guidelines to carefully cut out the rectangles through all layers. Remove the clips and erase any pencil marks (fig 69.5).

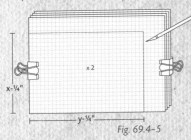

Fig. 69.4–5

6 Fold the stack in half and crease the fold with the side of the ruler (fig. 69.6).

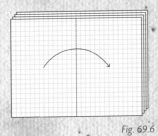

Fig. 69.6

7 With the right side out, fold the front panel in half. Fold the flap over the front, and use the pencil to make a small mark on the front panel on either side of the tab (fig. 69.7).

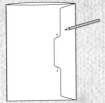

Fig. 69.7

8 Open the front panel flat again and cut a straight line connecting the two marks. You can insert the tab on the box flap into the slit to close the notebook (fig. 69.8).

Fig. 69.8

9 Open the folded papers and insert them into the fold (the spine) of the cardboard cover. Clip them together to keep them from shifting (fig. 69.9).

10 Use the sewing machine to carefully stitch a straight line along the spine, through the cover and the pages (fig. 69.10). Remove the clips and fold up the notebook.

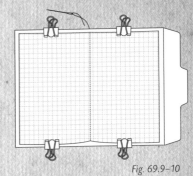

Fig. 69.9–10

Off-the-Record Notebook

- Craft knife
- 1 old record sleeve
- Ruler
- Pencil
- Self-healing cutting mat
- 50 pieces of scrap paper (at least 6" × 8") for the pages
- 2 binder clips
- 2 C-clamps
- Piece of wood
- Awl
- Hammer
- Waxed linen thread or embroidery floss
- Long sewing needle

LEVEL ✪ ✪ ✪ ✪ ✪

The ancient method of stab binding was commonly used in China and Japan many years before the modern codex binding we know today. Instead of trying to conceal the binding, this method makes it a feature in the book design. Old record album covers make sturdy notebook covers and are pretty easy to find at thrift shops. If you are a purist, use a cover that no longer has its record friend.

1 Use the craft knife to slit the top and bottom edge of the album cover. Open it up and lay it flat.

2 Use the ruler and pencil to measure and mark two 6" × 8" rectangles on the record cover. Use the craft knife and a cutting mat to cut out the rectangles (fig. 70.2).

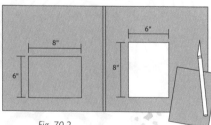

Fig. 70.2

3 Measure and mark a 6" × 8" rectangle on the top sheet of the scrap paper pages. Using the top sheet as a guide, and clamping about twelve sheets together at a time with the two binder clips, cut

out the rectangles. Repeat until all fifty sheets have been cut and remove the clips (fig. 70.3).

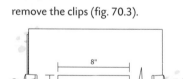

Fig. 70.3

4 Orient the front cover vertically, and lay it right side down.

5 Measure and mark a vertical line ¾" from the left side. Use the craft knife to gently score this line (fig. 70.5).

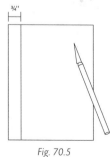

Fig. 70.5

6 Measure and mark a vertical line ³⁄₈" from the same edge. Don't score this line. Instead, along this line, measure and mark ½" from the top, ½" from the bottom, 1¾" from the top, 3" from the top, and 4¼" from the top (fig. 70.6).

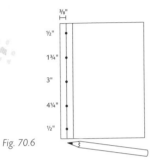

Fig. 70.6

7 Repeat steps 4 and 5 for the back cover.

8 Clamp the two covers together, right sides in, lining up the scored ends, and place the covers on the piece of wood. Use the awl and the hammer to punch through the marks you made in step 6 (fig. 70.8).

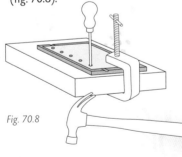

Fig. 70.8

9 On the top sheet of the vertically oriented pages, measure and mark a vertical line ³⁄₈" from the left edge of the paper. Along this line, measure and mark ½" from the top, ½" from the bottom, 1¾" from the top, 3" from the top, and 4¼" from the top (fig. 70.9).

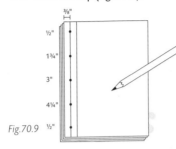

Fig. 70.9

10 Clamp the pages together, place them on the wood, and use an awl and hammer to pierce through the marks you made in step 9 (fig. 70.10).

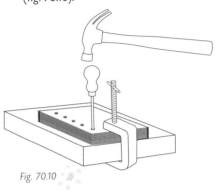

Fig. 70.10

⑪ Clamp the covers around the pages and line up all of the holes. Test that they are aligned by sticking the awl through each hole. If the awl goes cleanly through to the other side, you are ready to bind the book.

⑫ To bind the book, cut a 32" length of thread or floss and thread it though the needle.

⑬ Push the needle through the book from the bottom of the second hole to the top, leaving a 4" tail (fig. 70.13).

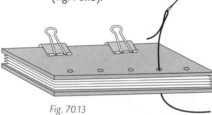

Fig. 70.13

⑭ Use your fingers to split the stack of book pages at about halfway, and use the awl to pull the tail out through the pages, pulling it taut so that it's hidden in the middle of the stack. Make a triple overhand knot at the end of the 4" tail (fig. 70.14).

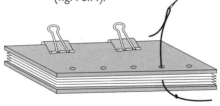

Fig. 70.14

⑮ Continue to bind, following the stitch order in the illustrations until you reach the final hole (fig. 70.15a–d).

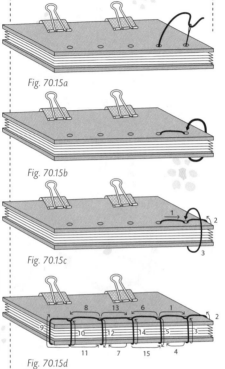

Fig. 70.15a

Fig. 70.15b

Fig. 70.15c

Fig. 70.15d

⑯ To finish off the thread, pass the needle up through the first stitch hole, under the two threads that extend from it, and make a loop (fig. 70.16a). Pass the needle through the loop to make an overhand knot, then back down through the same hole. Trim the excess thread (fig. 70.16b).

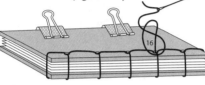

Fig. 70.16a

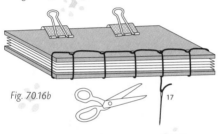

Fig. 70.16b

71 | Quilt Squares Photo Album

LEVEL ⊗⊗⊗⊗⊗

Okay, as you can probably tell, I am pretty frugal when it comes to craft supplies under all but a few very specific circumstances. This is one of those circumstances. A photo album should be made with the assumption that it will last for many years to come, and a lot of care should be taken with the construction and the craft. While white glue and scrap paper will usually do, I am going to suggest you use pH-neutral glue and acid-free paper for this project. The paper scrap cover mimics the top of an heirloom quilt; like a handsewn quilt, this album can be passed down from generation to generation.

WHAT YOU NEED

- 16 sheets of acid-free paper for the pages
- 2 sheets of acid-free paper in another color for the cover sheets
- Ruler
- Pencil
- 4 binder clips
- Craft knife
- Self-healing cutting mat
- ¼" circle hole punch
- Noncorrugated cardboard
- Paper for the cover and the lining of the album
- Small foam brush
- pH-neutral glue
- Linen hinging tape
- Small scraps (at least 4" × 4") of decorative paper for the "quilt" in equal amounts of warm and cool tones
- C-clamp
- 7"-long two-by-four piece of wood
- Drill with a ¼" boring bit
- Two ⅝" screw posts

1 Layer the 16 sheets of paper with a cover sheet on the top and bottom. Use the ruler and pencil to mark a 6½" × 10½" rectangle on the top sheet. Line up the pages and clamp them on opposite sides with binder clips (fig. 71.1).

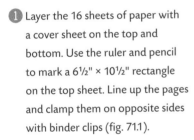

Fig. 71.1

2 Use the craft knife and cutting mat to cut out the marked rectangle through all the sheets of paper.

3 Unclip the paper. Orient the pile horizontally and, on the top sheet, measure and draw a vertical line 1½" from the left edge. Measure and mark a dot 1" down from the top of the page and 1" up from the bottom. Punch a hole at both of these marks (fig. 71.3).

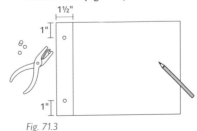

Fig. 71.3

4 Using the top sheet as a guide, punch holes through every sheet of paper.

5 Measure and cut two 11" × 7" and two 1½" × 7" pieces of cardboard. Then cut two 15" × 9" rectangles from the cover paper to cover the cardboard pieces. Last, cut two 6½" × 12" rectangles of paper to use as the cover lining (fig. 71.5a–c).

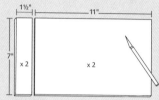

Fig. 71.5a

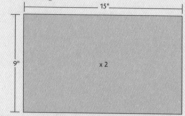

Fig. 71.5b

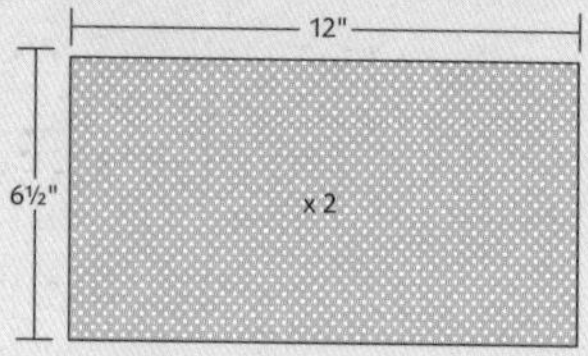

Fig. 71.5c

6 To make the front cover, lay one of the cover paper pieces right side down. Brush glue over one side of one 11" × 7" piece and one 1½" × 7" piece of cardboard. Leaving a 1" allowance, lay the pieces end to end on the cover paper with a ⅜" space in between (fig. 71.6).

Fig. 71.6

7 Cut a 7" length of tape and place it over the paper between the two pieces of cardboard, overlapping the edges of the cardboard slightly and connecting the two pieces (fig. 71.7).

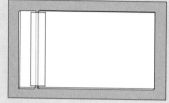

Fig. 71.7

8 Cut a diagonal at each corner of the paper (fig. 71.8).

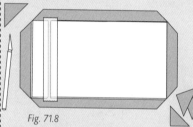

Fig. 71.8

9 Brush glue along the paper edges, and starting with the short sides of the paper, fold and press them over the edges of the cardboard cover (fig. 71.9).

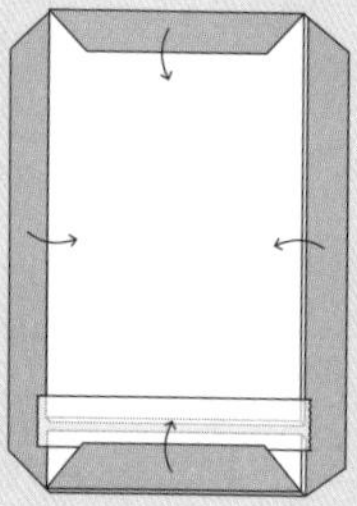

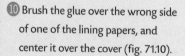

Fig. 71.9

10 Brush the glue over the wrong side of one of the lining papers, and center it over the cover (fig. 71.10).

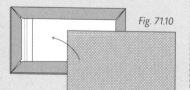

Fig. 71.10

11 Repeat steps 6 through 10 to make the back cover. Set aside the covers to dry.

12 Measure and cut twelve 1½" squares from the warm color scrap papers and twelve 1½" squares from the cool color scrap papers. Cut each of the 24 squares in half on the diagonal to make 48 triangles (fig. 71.12).

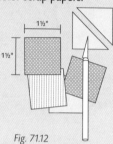

Fig. 71.12

13 Brush the back of a warm color triangle with the glue and arrange and press it into one corner of the front cover, leaving a ⅛" margin from the edge. Select a cool color triangle and arrange and glue it so it completes the square with the first triangle, leaving a 1/16" space along the diagonal that divides the square (fig. 71.13).

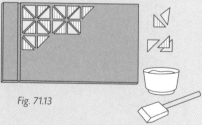

Fig. 71.13

14 Continue gluing down triangles, alternating warm and cool colors and following the pattern and spacing depicted in the illustration above. Repeat on the back cover. Let dry.

15 Using the holes in one of the interior book pages (from step 1) as a guide, mark the position for the holes along the small hinged margin on the inside of the front cover. Center the interior book page vertically and about ⅛" in from the edge of the cover (fig. 71.15).

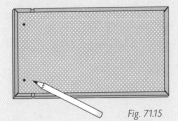

Fig. 71.15

16 Clamp the cover to the piece of wood and drill through the two marked dots to create holes (fig. 71.16).

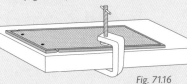

Fig. 71.16

17 Repeat steps 15 and 16 to prepare the back cover.

18 Use the screw posts and follow the illustration to assemble the photo album (fig. 71.18).

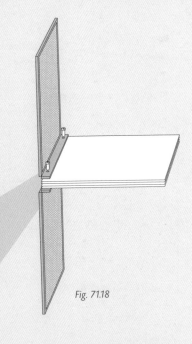

Fig. 71.18

72 | Signed, Sealed, Delivered Accordion Book

LEVEL ⊗⊗⊗⊗⊗

WHAT YOU NEED

- *6 envelopes of the same size*
- *Glue stick*
- *2 pieces of paper, each 2" longer and wider than the cardboard pieces below*
- *Hot glue gun and glue*
- *2 pieces of cardboard, each ½" wider and longer than envelopes*
- *Scissors*
- *Small scraps of paper in different colors (optional)*
- *2"-wide piece of ribbon*

This accordion book is the perfect way to organize all the little bits of paper that clutter up your wallet: to-do lists, receipts, business cards, recipes, and coupons. Or make an accordion scrapbook to hold all your remembrances from a trip: train tickets, museum passes, foreign stamps, and more!

1 Open the flap of one of the envelopes and lay it flat, open side up.

2 Spread glue stick over the inside of the flap. Open the flap of a second envelope and line up its bottom edge with the fold of the first envelope flap (fig. 72.2). Press it down to stick.

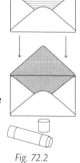
Fig. 72.2

3 Repeat step 2 with the remaining four envelopes.

4 For the last envelope, fold the flap back and glue it to the front of the envelope (fig. 72.4). Set the chain of envelopes aside.

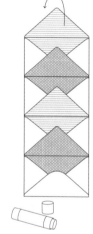
Fig. 72.4

5 Lay one of the pieces of paper right side down, quickly spread hot glue over one side of a cardboard piece, and center and press down onto the paper.

6 Cut a diagonal at each corner of the paper (fig. 72.6).

Fig. 72.6

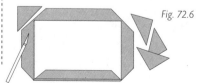

7 Squeeze a line of hot glue along each edge of paper and fold and press it over the edge of the cardboard (fig. 72.7a). *Optional:* Cut a few strips of scrap paper and glue them to the front of the covered cardboard with a glue stick. Fold the ends of the papers over the edges of the cardboard and glue them (fig. 72.7b).

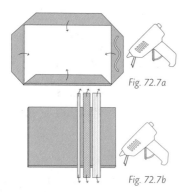

Fig. 72.7a

Fig. 72.7b

8 Repeat steps 5 through 7 with the second piece of paper and cardboard to complete the second cover of the book.

9 Quickly spread hot glue over the front side of the first envelope in the envelope chain from step 4. Center and press it onto the wrong side of one of the cardboard covers (fig. 72.9).

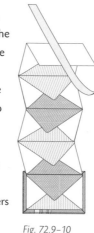

Fig. 72.9–10

10 Squeeze a few dots of glue at the center along the right side of the ribbon. Center the ribbon across the last envelope and press it down (fig. 72.10).

11 Spread hot glue over the envelope and ribbon and center and press it onto the wrong side of the second cardboard cover (fig. 72.11). *Note:* Check that the two cardboard covers are aligned.

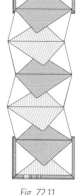

Fig. 72.11

12 Tie the ends of the ribbon across the front cover in a knot or bow.

Do Me a Favor Box, page 204

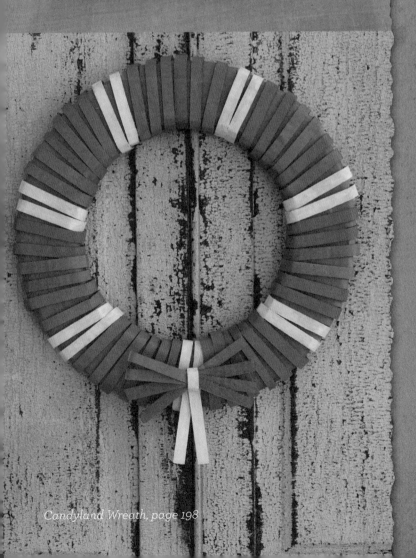

Candyland Wreath, page 198

six

PAPER FOR
PARTIES

WHAT YOU NEED

(makes 1 pom-pom)

- *16 sheets of tissue paper in desired color*
- *Scissors*
- *White floral wire*
- *Wire cutters*
- *Cotton thread for hanging (optional)*

Pleats Please Me

Japanese design company Nendo was asked by fashion designer Issey Miyake to create a chair from a very unconventional material, a by-product of his Pleats Please line: When fabric is pleated, it is done on paper. Usually this paper gets tossed when the pleating is complete, but Nendo turned a roll of pleated sheets into a layered paper chair (www .nendo.jp/en/works/detail .php?y=2008&t=111). The result starts out like a tight roll of paper and, as you peel back the paper layers, ends up somewhat resembling a Lhasa apso.

73 | Paper Poms

LEVEL ⦿ ⦿ ⦿ ⦿ ⦿

When my friends threw me a bridal shower a few years ago, they decorated the party space with these light-as-air, ethereal pom-poms. They were such a hit that we made tons more for our wedding reception. They're simple and inexpensive to make, but when hung en masse they look like a million bucks and transform pretty much any place into a poofy fantasyland.

---

1 Stack eight sheets of tissue paper, lining up the edges. Starting at one of the shorter edges, make 1½" accordion folds, creasing at each fold, until you reach the opposite edge (fig. 73.1).

Fig. 73.1

2 Find the center of the folded strip and cut a small V-shaped notch into each folded edge, through all layers (fig. 73.2).

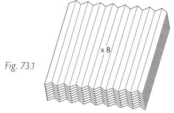

Fig. 73.2

3 Use wire cutters to cut a 10" piece of floral wire and wrap it around the center of the folded strips, at the notches. Twist the wire to secure it.

Trim a point or rounded edge at each end of the folded strip (fig. 73.3). (If you are making a lot of pom-poms, try some of both!)

Fig. 73.3

4 Repeat steps 1 through 3 (this will be the second half of the pom-pom).

5 Open the accordion folds on both poms and *carefully* pull each layer of the pom-pom away from the center (fig. 73.5).

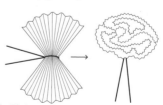

Fig. 73.5

6 Twist together the wires of both halves of the pom-pom, fluff up the pom-pom again, and then bend the wire into a loop for hanging (fig. 73.6). *Optional:* Tie thread through the loop for more flexibility in hanging.

Fig. 73.6

WHAT YOU NEED

- Access to a computer with a printer and paper

- Paper doll, tree, flower, heart, and other garland templates*

- Craft knife

- Self-healing cutting mat

- Ruler

- Newspaper (or magazine) pages

- Pencil

- Scissors

- Hot glue gun and glue (optional)

74 | Paper Chain, Chain, Chain

LEVEL ⊗ ⊗ ⊗ ⊗ ⊗

Nothing transports me back to childhood like cutting paper doll chains. Channel your inner kid and make a whole bunch of these to hang as garlands at a party. I've provided templates for a paper doll, tree, flower, heart, and a few other designs to get you started. *Note:* The craft knife provides more precise cutting, but if you decide to share the fun and actually make these with kids, skip the craft knife and use a pair of scissors.

* Download at workman.com/papermade

1. Print the paper doll, tree, flower, heart, or other garland template and cut it out using a craft knife and cutting mat.

2. Cut a strip of newspaper 5" long and use the width of the paper (fig. 74.2).

Fig. 74.2

3. Place the left edge of the template at the left edge of the paper strip and trace around the template.

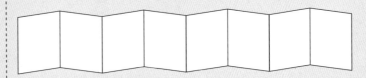

Fig. 74.5

4. Make the first accordion fold at the right edge of the paper template tracing.

Fig. 74.6

5. Continue folding the paper strip, accordion-style, for the length of the strip (fig. 74.5). Trim off any excess flaps of paper.

6. Cut along the marked lines of the template tracing, through all layers (fig. 74.6).

Fig. 74.7

7. Unfold the chain carefully (fig. 74.7). *Optional:* To extend the garland, repeat steps 1 through 6 to create more chains, then hot glue each chain together.

Whirling, Twirling Ornaments

LEVEL ✪ ✪ ✪ ✪ ✪

WHAT YOU NEED
· · · · · · · · · · · · · · · · · ·

(makes 3 ornaments)

- *Access to a computer with a printer and paper*
- *Ornament templates**
- *Craft knife*
- *Self-healing cutting mat*
- *6 sheets of decorative paper (10" × 10") in contrasting colors, for the front and back of the ornament*
- *3 sheets of 10" × 10" card stock*
- *4 binder clips*
- *Pencil*
- *Glue stick*
- *Sewing thread*

There's just something about vintage ornaments that gets me every time. I like their faded colors, but what I really love are their shapes. Today's Christmas balls have nothing on the sinuous and sophisticated vintage silhouettes. This twirling ornament takes the essence of the ornament shape and makes it modern and geometric. Imagine how great a cluster of them would look hanging off a branch over a dining room table or from a window frame.

1 Print out the ornament templates and cut them out using a craft knife and cutting mat.

2 Lay one sheet of decorative paper facedown on the mat. Layer the sheet of card stock on top, followed by the second sheet of decorative paper, faceup (fig. 75.2).

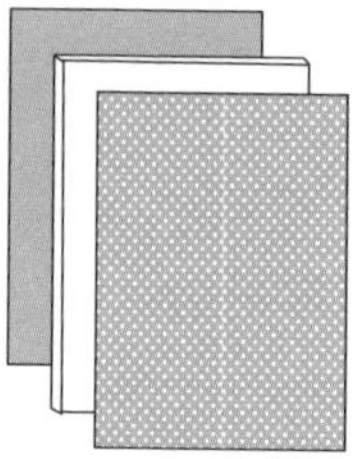

Fig. 75.2

3 Use the binder clips to secure the pile on all four sides. Arrange the templates on the top sheet of paper and use the pencil to trace around them (fig. 75.3).

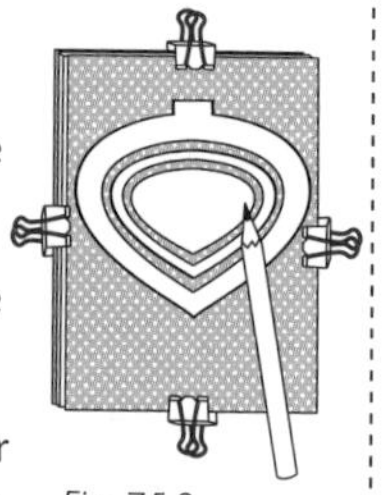

Fig. 75.3

4 Cut along the traced lines through all three layers.

5 Spread glue stick on one side of all the card stock pieces and press them one at a time onto the wrong side of their matching decorative pieces. *Note:* You should have four decorative pieces remaining (fig. 75.5).

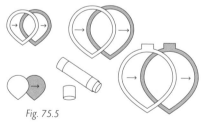

Fig. 75.5

6 Lay out the glued pieces to form the concentric pieces of the ornament with the card stock sides facing up. Then spread glue stick over each of the card stock pieces.

* Download at workman.com/papermade

7 Cut a long piece of thread and line it up so it runs vertically through the center of the card stock pieces. Press it into the glue (fig. 75.7).

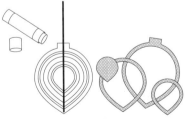

Fig. 75.7

8 Select the remaining pieces of decorative paper and layer them over the thread, lining them up with their respective card stock pieces. Press down along the center of the ornament to seal in the thread (fig. 75.8). Let dry.

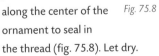

Fig. 75.8

9 Repeat steps 1 through 8 for the remaining two ornaments.

(makes 1 fan)

- Access to a computer with a printer and paper

- Fan, hearts, and vines templates*

- Craft knife

- Self-healing cutting mat

- 2 sheets of colored paper, for front and back of fan

- Pencil

- Foam brush

- Acid-free paper glue

- Paper packaging cardboard

- Scraps of decorative paper for details

- Typewriter, calligraphy pen, or other writing material (optional)

- Hot glue gun and glue

- Large wood craft stick

* Download at workman.com/papermade

76 | I'm Your Number 1 Fan

LEVEL ✖ ✖ ✖ ✖ ✖

Handheld fans are elegant—and very appreciated—favors at humid, outdoor summer weddings or other family affairs. This one can be personalized with the event date so it can be treasured as a keepsake. Make sure to save one for yourself!

① Print the fan and fan decoration templates and cut them out using the craft knife and cutting mat.

② Select the sheet of colored paper for the front of the fan, and use the pencil to trace the fan template onto it four times, rotating and flipping the template along the straight edges to complete the shape. Then roughly cut out about 1" around the traced shape (fig. 76.2).

Fig. 76.2

③ Brush acid-free paper glue over the back of the paper shape and press it onto a piece of cardboard (fig. 76.3). Let dry.

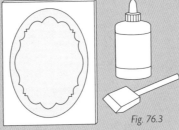

Fig. 76.3

④ Use the craft knife to carefully cut around the traced shape through both layers (fig. 76.4).

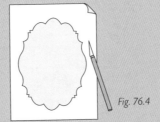

Fig. 76.4

⑤ Brush glue over the cardboard side and press it onto the second sheet of colored paper. Let dry and trim the excess paper from the back of the fan.

⑥ Select scrap papers for the hearts and vines. Trace the hearts and vines templates and cut them out (fig. 76.6). *Optional:* Type, handwrite, or draw calligraphy on one of the hearts to personalize it.

Fig. 76.6

⑦ Brush the backs of the hearts and vines with glue and arrange as desired on the fan.

⑧ Squeeze a 3" line of hot glue along one end of the wood craft stick and press it, centered, onto the bottom back of the fan as the handle (fig. 76.8). *Optional:* Type, handwrite, or draw a little saying in calligraphy ("I'm your biggest fan") on a small paper scrap. Cut it into a strip, and glue it to the handle of the fan.

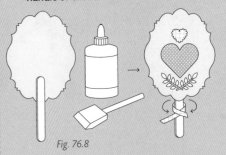

Fig. 76.8

WHAT YOU NEED

(makes at least 3 wrappers)

- *Access to a computer with a printer and paper*
- *Cupcake wrapper templates**
- *Craft knife*
- *Self-healing cutting mat*
- *Pencil*
- *Colored paper*
- *Small paintbrush*
- *White glue*
- *Cupcakes*

77 | Take the Cake Cupcake Wrappers

LEVEL ⊗ ⊗ ⊗ ⊗ ⊗

Cupcakes, as small as they are, pack a mean punch of perfection. With all the cupcake love sweeping the nation, here's a project that helps you go the extra mile for your home-baked goodies. These decorative wrappers are the icing on the cake, so to speak, of your favorite cupcake recipe.

---

1 Print the cupcake wrapper templates and cut them out using a craft knife and cutting mat.

2 Use the pencil to trace one of the templates onto colored paper. Cut around the tracings and erase any stray pencil marks (fig. 77.2).

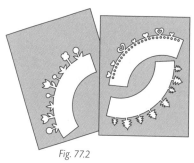

Fig. 77.2

3 Wrap the paper around the cupcake to make sure it fits well. Trim it if necessary. Remove the wrapper from the cupcake, pinching it together where the edges overlap, and secure the overlap with a bit of white glue (fig. 77.3).

Fig. 77.4

4 Repeat steps 2 and 3 to complete the remaining wrappers. Let dry before inserting cupcakes (fig. 77.5)!

Fig. 77.5

* Download at workman.com/papermade

WHAT YOU NEED

· · · · · · · · · · · · · · · · · · · ·

(makes 2 prize balls)

- A roll of crepe paper party streamers (makes about three balls) in red and orange

- Scissors

- Tiny toys or candies (select a few "larger" ones and some small, flat treats)

- Hot glue gun and glue

- Pencil

- 3" square piece of green crepe paper or other lightweight paper

78 | **Apples to Oranges Surprise Balls**

LEVEL ⊗ ⊗ ⊗ ⊗ ⊗

Surprise! These crepe paper apples and oranges might look like they're just (seriously cute) decorations, but your party guests will be delighted to find all sorts of surprises hidden inside: toys, candy, confetti, love notes, fortunes . . . a few little delights that equal a lot of fun.

1. Unroll the streamer about 2 yards and cut lengthwise down the middle with scissors to create two narrower streamer strips (fig. 78.1).

Fig. 78.1

2. Continue cutting lengthwise until you've cut into about one third of the roll. Snip off the strips.

3. Select several larger toys, cluster them together, and start wrapping one of the strips around the toys (fig. 78.3).

Fig. 78.3

4. Wrap the bundle several times to create a somewhat round shape (fig. 78.4).

Fig. 78.4

5. Add a smaller treat to the outside of the bundle and continue wrapping (fig. 78.5).

Fig. 78.5

6. Continue rolling, wrapping new treats into the outer layers until your ball is roughly the size of an apple or orange. Secure the end of the streamer to the ball with hot glue (fig. 78.6).

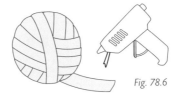

Fig. 78.6

For the orange

7. Draw and cut one ½"-long leaf from the green crepe paper. Fold it in half (fig. 78.7).

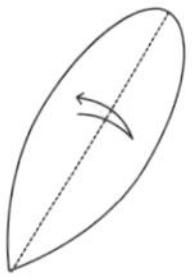

Fig. 78.7

8. Cut a 1½" × 3" strip of crepe paper. Cut ½" fringe into one long edge of the strip and roll up the strip to make a 1½" stem. Squeeze a dab of hot glue to secure the end of the strip (fig. 78.8).

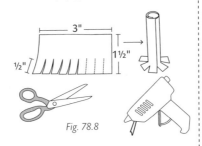

Fig. 78.8

9. Fan out the fringe on the bottom of the stem and glue and press the fringe to the top of the orange surprise ball (fig. 78.9).

10. Glue the leaf to the stem at the base (fig. 78.10).

Fig. 78.9–10

For the apple

7. Draw and cut two 1"-long leaves from the green crepe paper. Fold them in half (fig. 78.7a).

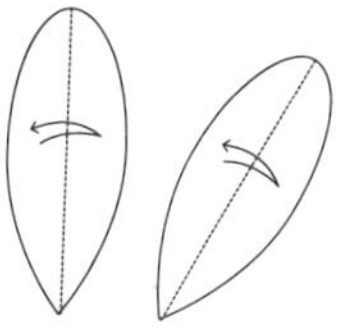

Fig. 78.7a

8. Cut a 1" × 3" strip of crepe paper and roll up the strip to make a 1" stem. Squeeze a dab of hot glue to secure the end of the strip (fig. 78.8a).

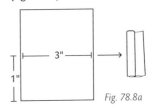

Fig. 78.8a

9. Use your finger to make an indent at the top of the ball to form the apple (fig. 78.9a).

Fig. 78.9a

10. Dot the bottom of the 1" stem with hot glue and secure it, centered, in the indent at the top of the apple surprise ball. Glue the leaves around the stem (fig. 78.10a).

Fig. 78.10a

O Happy Day Banner

LEVEL ⊗⊗⊗⊗⊗

WHAT YOU NEED

- *Access to a computer with a printer and paper*
- *Triangular and rounded pennant and letter templates**
- *Scissors*
- *Pencil*
- *Assorted papers (at least 6" × 10")*
- *Decorative-edge scissors*
- *Glue stick*
- *String*

I'm sure you've seen banners that spell out common sentiments like Happy Birthday or Congratulations or It's a Girl!, but what about a banner that just celebrates any old day? I love the idea of sending this to a friend or a loved one as a greeting card. You can even personalize the banner. I used little saved scraps of wallpaper, card stock, and origami paper left over from other projects to make the banner and the letters. You can use any kind of paper you have lying around. Magazines, newspapers, wrapping paper, and junk mail all make for a very festive banner indeed.

1 Print the triangular and rounded pennant and letter templates and cut them out using scissors.

2 Use the pencil to trace the letters onto different papers. Cut them out with scissors and erase any stray pencil marks (fig. 79.2). Set them aside.

3 Fold a piece of scrap paper in half, place the short edge of one of the pennant templates along the fold line, and trace it. Repeat to trace seven triangular pennants and eight rounded pennants in all.

4 Use the decorative-edge scissors to cut out the pennants (fig. 79.4). Erase any stray pencil marks.

Fig. 79.2

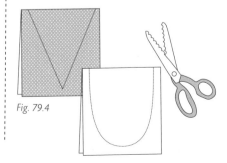

Fig. 79.4

✿
Waste Not, Want Not

The average office worker in the United States uses ten thousand sheets of copy paper each year. That's four million tons of copy paper used annually! Why not reuse some of that paper for good and try some paper crafting?

* Download at workman.com/papermade

5 Keeping them folded over (so the banner will be double-sided), lay out three triangle pennants, five rounded pennants, one triangle pennant, three rounded pennants, and three triangle pennants in rows (fig. 79.5).

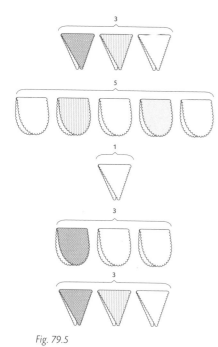

Fig. 79.5

6 Use glue stick to attach a letter to each of the rounded pennants (fig. 79.6).

Fig. 79.6

7 Cut an 80" length of string. Spread glue stick over only the inner fold of the first pennant. Leaving 10" at one end, insert the string into the fold (fig. 79.7).

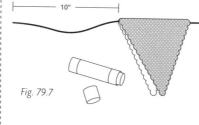

Fig. 79.7

8 Repeat step 7 to add each pennant to the string, evenly spacing them about 2" apart (fig. 79.8).

Fig. 79.8

80 | Snap, Crackle, Popper!

LEVEL ⦿⦿⊗⊗⊗

Crackers have been a traditional part of British Christmas festivities and other celebrations since Victorian times. Because two people have to open a cracker together, and because it is absolutely impossible not to squeal with delight when you pull one open with a loud *pop!*, it's a great way to get a party started. (That, of course, and champagne!) If you want to do it right (and by that I mean the proper British way), fill the crackers with a couple of small toys, a typed message or joke, and a paper crown. And yes, you do have to wear the paper crown after you open the cracker—it just adds to the good silly fun of the whole thing.

1. Measure the length of the cracker snap and add ½" (*x*). Measure the circumference of the toilet paper roll and add 1" (*y*). Then mark and cut an *x*" by *y*" rectangle of kraft paper. Mark and cut an (*x*"−1½") by *y*" rectangle of tissue paper (fig. 80.1).

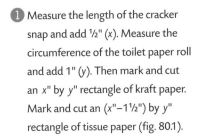
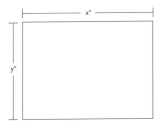

Fig. 80.1

2. Trim the edges of both rectangles with the decorative edge scissors.

3. Center the toilet paper roll along one long edge of the kraft paper. Squeeze a line of hot glue equal to the length of the toilet paper roll along the edge of the kraft paper width and attach the roll to the paper (fig. 80.3).

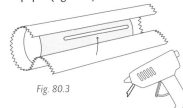

Fig. 80.3

4. Roll up the toilet paper roll in the kraft paper and squeeze a line of hot glue along the opposite edge of the paper to secure it.

WHAT YOU NEED

(makes 1 cracker)

- Ruler
- 1 cracker snap (see Resources, page 10, for where to order)
- Toilet paper roll
- Pencil
- Kraft paper
- Tissue paper in a few colors
- Scissors
- Decorative-edge scissors
- Hot glue gun and glue
- Ribbon
- Small toys
- Typed or handwritten joke or fortune

5 Thread the cracker snap through the roll and center it so that the ends are visible on both sides of the roll.

6 Twist the kraft paper tightly at one end of the roll (with the snap end enclosed) and tie around the twist with ribbon (fig. 80.6). Set it aside.

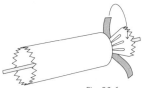

Fig. 80.6

7 Cut a 3" × 24" strip of tissue paper. Form it into a loop and secure the ends with a line of hot glue (fig. 80.7).

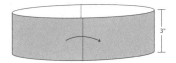

Fig. 80.7

8 Flatten the loop and fold it in half twice. Cut a reverse V shape into one of the cut edges to make the top of the crown (fig. 80.8). *Optional:* If the traditional zigzag shape seems too pedestrian, cut more intricate shapes into the edge.

Fig. 80.8

9 Insert the folded crown into the open end of the toilet paper tube. Add a couple of favors and a joke or fortune (fig. 80.9).

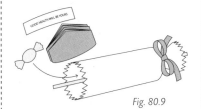

Fig. 80.9

10 Twist the kraft paper tightly to close up the roll and tie it with ribbon. Make sure you can still easily reach the cracker snap on both ends.

11 Starting at one short end, accordion-fold the tissue paper rectangle every ½" (fig. 80.11).

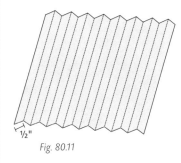

½"

Fig. 80.11

12 Use the paper scissors to snip little shapes along the folded edges (fig. 80.12).

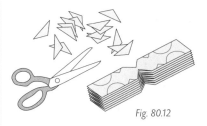

Fig. 80.12

13 Unfold the tissue paper and wrap it around the center of the cracker. Squeeze a line of hot glue to secure the ends (fig. 80.13).

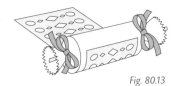

Fig. 80.13

81 | Piece of (Cup)cake Paper Flower

LEVEL ✪ ✪ ✪ ✪ ✪

If you've ever baked in your life, you probably have a box of cupcake liners stuffed somewhere at the back of a shelf in your pantry. Rather than holding out for the next time you have a moment to bake (c'mon, they're already gathering dust!), use a few of those cupcake liners to make these ridiculously cute gift toppers.

WHAT YOU NEED

- *12 cupcake liners*
- *Sewing needle*
- *6" thin wire*
- *Pencil*
- *Scissors*
- *Small scraps of green tissue paper or card stock*

❶ Make a stack of twelve cupcake liners and flatten them. Use the sewing needle to poke two holes about ½" apart through the bottom center of the layers of liners (fig. 81.1).

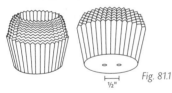

Fig. 81.1

❷ Thread the wire from back to front through one of the holes and all of the layers. Then thread the wire through the second hole from front to back. Even out the ends at the back and twist the ends once around each other (fig. 81.2).

Fig. 81.2

❸ Separate the cupcake liners one at a time, twisting each one slightly to make the flower nice and full (fig. 81.3).

Fig. 81.3

❹ Draw and cut two leaf shapes from the green tissue paper and pierce the wire ends through one point on each leaf. Twist the wire again to secure them (fig. 81.4).

Fig. 81.4

❺ Twist the ends of the wire to the ribbon on the top of a gift and trim the wire.

VARIATION

A bunch of these flowers makes a nice everlasting bouquet. Just cut longer lengths of wire for each flower and wrap the wires with floral tape to finish.

Not Afraid of My Shadow Puppets

LEVEL ● ● ● ○ ○

WHAT YOU NEED

(makes 4 different puppets)

- *Access to a computer with a printer and paper*
- *Shadow puppet templates**
- *Craft knife*
- *Self-healing cutting mat*
- *Pencil*
- *Black construction paper*
- *¼" hole punch*
- *Brads*
- *Hot glue gun and glue*
- *Wooden skewers*

According to legend, shadow puppetry was born after a beloved concubine of Emperor Wu of Han died from an illness in 88 B.C. The emperor was devastated by the loss, and he summoned his court officers to bring his beloved back to life. The officers cut out a silhouette of the concubine from donkey leather and, using an oil lamp for light, they made her shadow move, thus "bringing her back to life." The art of shadow puppetry has endured many years and in very different cultures. Today its appeal is in its distance from most modern forms of entertainment—it's a chance for friends and families to turn off the TV, spend time together, and be creative.

1 Print the shadow puppet templates and cut them out using the craft knife and cutting mat.

2 Trace the template pieces on black construction paper and cut around the tracings (fig. 82.2).

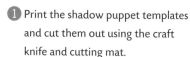

Fig. 82.2

* Download at workman.com/papermade

③ Using the templates as a guide, punch holes in the joints of each animal (fig. 82.3).

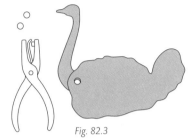

Fig. 82.3

④ Connect the pieces by inserting brads into the holes and opening the prongs to secure them (fig. 82.4).

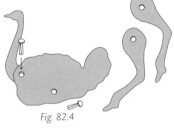

Fig. 82.4

⑤ One at a time, squeeze hot glue 2" along the end of each skewer and press it onto the back of the shadow puppets (use the illustrations and photos as guides to determine placement—each puppet requires two to three skewers) (fig. 82.5).

Fig. 82.5

- *Access to a computer with a printer and paper*
- *Banner template**
- *Craft knife*
- *Self-healing cutting mat*
- *¼" hole punch*
- *⅛" hole punch*
- *Ruler*
- *Zigzag-edge scissors*
- *Tissue paper in three colors*
- *Pencil*
- *Glue stick*
- *String or twine*

83 | Papel Picado Flags

LEVEL ✖ ✖ ✖ ✖ ✖

Like pretty much every culture around the globe, Mexico has a rich tradition of elaborate paper cutting. *Papel picado* is cut primarily from tissue paper and features themes including birds, flowers, and skeletons. *Papel picado* flags are displayed at Easter, Day of the Dead, and Christmas celebrations as well as weddings, *quinceañeras*, and baptisms. Hang a few *papel picado* banners at your next celebratory occasion, too!

① Print the banner template and cut it out with the craft knife and cutting mat (fig. 83.1). Use the hole punches to cut out the small circles.

Fig. 83.1

② Measure and use the zigzag scissors to cut out five 10" × 13" pieces from one tissue paper color (fig. 83.2).

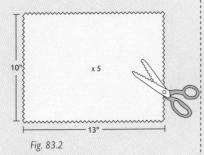

x 5

10"

13"

Fig. 83.2

③ Fold each rectangle in half widthwise to make five 10" × 6½" rectangles (fig. 83.3).

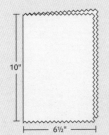

10"

6½"

Fig. 83.3

④ Cut two 6" × 9" rectangles from one of the other tissue paper

colors and three 6" × 9" rectangles from the third (fig. 83.4).

6"

9"

Fig. 83.4

⑤ Fold all five rectangles in half widthwise (fig. 83.5).

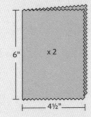

6"

x 2

x 3

4½"

Fig. 83.5

⑥ Line up the straight edge of the banner template along one of the folded edges of the rectangles from step 3. Trace the design with a pencil (fig. 83.6).

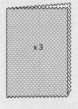

Fig. 83.6

⑦ Cut out along the marked lines through both layers. Use the hole punches to cut out the small circles (fig. 83.7).

Fig. 83.7

⑧ Repeat steps 6 and 7 to trace and cut out the other four banner pieces.

⑨ Spread glue stick over the back of each cut tissue paper piece and glue it to one side of the rectangles cut in step 2 (fig. 83.9).

Fig. 83.9

⑩ Cut a 90" piece of string. Lay out the banners and spread glue stick over the inside fold of the larger rectangles. Leaving 10" of string at one end, press the string into the glued folds of the paper banners, evenly spacing the banner pieces about 5" apart (fig. 83.10).

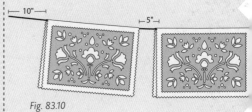

10"

5"

Fig. 83.10

* Download at workman.com/papermade

Candyland Wreath

- *Ruler*
- *Box cutter*
- *Self-healing cutting mat*
- *Medium cardboard box (about 18" × 18" × 16"), flattened*
- *Hot glue gun and glue*
- *16" foam wreath form*
- *Scissors*
- *Foam brush*
- *Craft paint in white and pink*

LEVEL ⊗ ⊗ ⊗ ⊗ ⊗

Though I wasn't graced with much of a sweet tooth, I have always been inspired by the way sweets look—color swirls, sugary sparkles, and crunchy clusters. Maybe that explains all the Candyland I played as a kid. I used to fantasize about what it would be like if Candy Cane Forests and Gumdrop Mountains were real! So it comes as no surprise that, when the holidays are approaching, I turn to candy to create a crafty wonderland. This wreath is inspired by one of the prettiest candies, in my opinion: the venerable Starlight Mint.

1 Use the ruler, box cutter, and cutting mat to cut thirty ¾" × 18" strips from the cardboard box. Make all cuts perpendicular to the direction of the corrugation (fig. 84.1).

Fig. 84.1

2 Select one strip and glue one end, centered on the back of the wreath form (fig. 84.2).

Fig. 84.2

3 Wrap the other end over the front and around to the back, then glue it to secure it. Trim the end of the strip with scissors if needed (fig. 84.3).

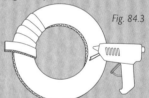

Fig. 84.3

4 Continue wrapping strips around the form until they cover it. Arrange the strips as closely together as possible so the form underneath is less visible (fig. 84.4). Set it aside.

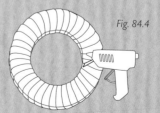

Fig. 84.4

⑤ Cut fifty-six ½" × 9" strips from the cardboard box. Make all cuts perpendicular to the direction of the corrugation.

⑥ Select fourteen strips and use the foam brush to paint just one side of each strip white. Paint twenty-eight strips pink, and leave the remaining fourteen natural (fig. 84.6). Let dry.

Fig. 84.6

⑦ Use the ½" × 9" strips to cover the "seams" left between the wrapped strips in step 4. Select a white strip and glue one end to the back of the form, wrap the other end over the front and around the back, and glue it to secure it. Repeat with two pink strips and then one natural strip to create a pattern (fig. 84.7).

Fig. 84.7

⑧ Repeat the pattern in Step 7 until all the strips have been used.

⑨ To make the bow, use the scissors to cut four ½" × 6" strips of cardboard. Bundle three of them together, then fan them out from the center and hot glue them. Cut a ½" × 2" strip of cardboard and wrap and hot glue it around the center of the fan (fig. 84.9).

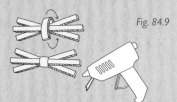

Fig. 84.9

⑩ Fold the fourth ½" × 9" strip in half at an angle and hot glue it to the back of the fan to form a bow (fig. 84.10).

Fig. 84.10

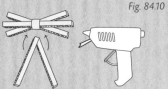

⑪ Apply hot glue to the back of the bow and attach it to the bottom of the wreath (fig. 84.11). Hang the completed wreath on a hook or nail.

Fig. 84.11

WHAT YOU NEED

(makes cover for 1 string of lights)

- Magazine pages
- String of LED lights
- Ruler
- Craft knife
- Self-healing cutting mat

85 | Starstruck String of Lights

LEVEL ✪ ✪ ✪ ✪ ✪

O rigami water balloons can actually hold water (hence the name), but let's steer clear of water when we use them as covers for strings of winking, blinking lights. String them up outside for an evening garden party or barbecue! I made these water balloon luminarias from old magazine pages—but newspaper, origami paper, or any other lightweight papers work equally as well.

❖
Astral Planes

I n 2008, a group of Japanese scientists planned to send a small fleet of paper planes to Earth from outer space, claiming that a well-folded paper plane could easily make the 250-mile trip back to Earth. They were probably right but had to abandon their plans after admitting that the planes would not only be impossible to track but would most likely land in water on their reentry into Earth's atmosphere.

1. Tear out a magazine page for every bulb on the string of lights. Use the ruler, craft knife, and cutting mat to trim them into squares, equal in dimension to the short side of the page.

2. Lay one square flat, right side up. Valley fold the square in half to make a rectangle. Unfold and valley fold in half in the other direction. Unfold (fig. 85.2).

Fig. 85.2

3. Mountain fold the paper diagonally to make a triangle. Unfold and mountain fold along the opposite diagonal. Unfold (fig. 85.3).

Fig. 85.3

4. Push in the valley folds (page 5) so they collapse inward to make a triangle shape (fig. 85.4).

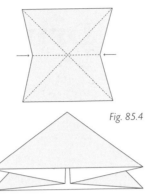

Fig. 85.4

5. Fold up the left and right front flaps of the triangular end to meet in the center (fig. 85.5). Flip the triangle over and repeat to complete a square, oriented as a diamond.

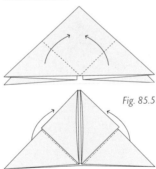

Fig. 85.5

6. Fold the left and right points in to the center crease, creating little triangular pockets (fig. 85.6). Flip the project over and repeat on the other side.

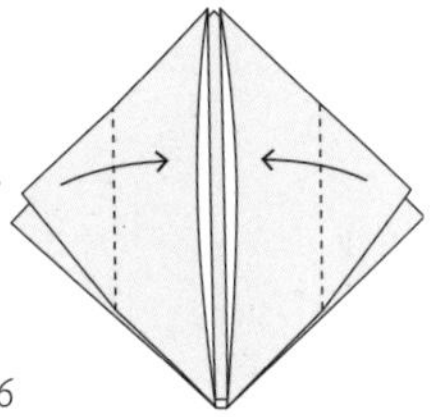

Fig. 85.6

7. Fold up the bottom flaps and tuck them neatly into the pockets (fig. 85.7). Flip the project over and repeat on the other side.

Fig. 85.7

8. There will be a small hole on the top side of the paper where the folds come together. Gently blow into it, and see a cube start to form. Ease the shape by opening some of the folds as you blow (fig. 85.8).

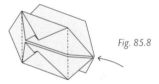

Fig. 85.8

9. Once the cube is formed, crease each side of the cube to neaten the structure.

10. Carefully fit each cube over a bulb on the string of lights (fig. 85.10).

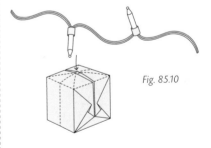

Fig. 85.10

It's Raining, It's Pouring Drink Umbrellas

LEVEL ✪ ✪ ✪ ✪ ✪

WHAT YOU NEED

- Pencil
- Ruler
- Scraps of paper (at least 3½" × 3½")
- Decorative-edge scissors
- Scissors
- Hot glue gun and glue
- Wooden skewers

When I was a kid, a big family treat included a night out for Chinese food. I liked the fortune cookies and the crispy noodles, but what I really loved were the drink umbrellas. I would sip my Shirley Temple or virgin Mai Tai and twirl my drink umbrella back and forth, back and forth. This is a supersimple project for making a summer dinner party feel extra festive and fun!

1 Draw or trace a 3" circle on a scrap of paper and use the decorative-edge scissors to cut it out (fig. 86.1).

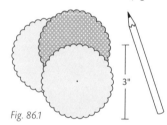

Fig. 86.1

2 Find the center of the circle and mark a line along the radius (from the center point to any point on the outside edge of the circle). Use regular scissors to cut along that line (fig. 86.2).

Fig. 86.2

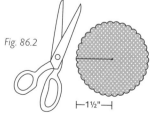

├─1½"─┤

3 Overlap the cut straight edges about ½" to form a shallow cone. Squeeze a thin line of hot glue along one edge of the cut circle, and secure the overlap (fig. 86.3).

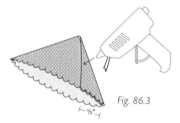

Fig. 86.3

├─ ½"─┤

4 Balance the umbrella on top of the wooden skewer, lining up the point of the skewer with the small hole at the top of the cone. Squeeze a few dots of glue on the inside to secure (fig. 86.4).

Fig. 86.4

(makes 1 lidded box)

- Two 6" x 6" sheets of lightweight paper (book pages, magazine pages, maps, and origami paper work well)

- Scissors

- Other scraps of paper, 1 at least 1" x 1" and another at least 2" x 6"

- Ruler

- Hot glue gun and glue

- 1" round hole punch

87 | Do Me a Favor Box

LEVEL ⬤⬤⬤✕✕

The custom of giving favor boxes at weddings is a sweet little tradition that marks the start of a couple's new life together. The celebration isn't just for the couple but for everyone present to make the wonderful day happen. These origami-style boxes are a way to deliver your thanks in a very personalized way: You can even use papers that have significance to you—maps that show your heritage, copies of pages from your favorite book or poem, an old event program.

1 Place one 6" x 6" sheet of paper in front of you right side down. Mountain fold in half once, open, and then mountain fold in half the other way. Open the sheet (fig. 87.1).

Fig. 87.1

2 Use the folds as your guides to valley fold the four corners of the sheet into the center to make a smaller square (fig. 87.2).

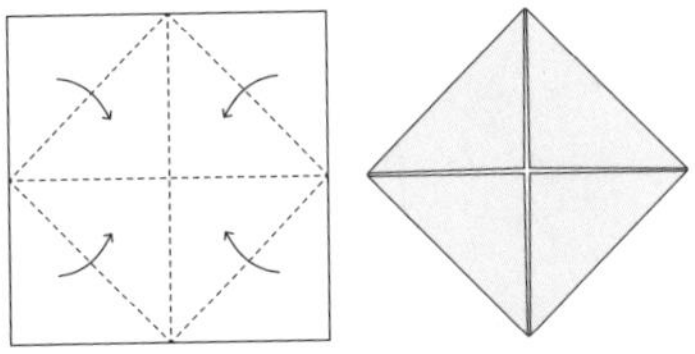

Fig. 87.2

3 One at a time, valley fold each folded edge into the center, crease, and unfold (fig. 87.3).

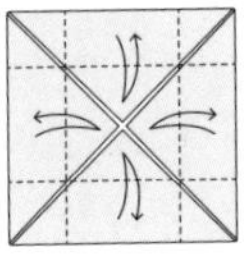

Fig. 87.3

4 Open out the top and bottom triangle flaps and then valley fold the left and right edge into the center (fig. 87.4).

Fig. 87.4

5 Valley fold the top point down diagonally to one side, crease, and then open up again (fig. 87.5). Repeat, folding and creasing on the opposite diagonal.

Fig. 87.5

6 Repeat step 5 on the bottom point.

7 Gently pull apart the folded center edges and fold and tuck the top corner into the center, pushing the sides of the box up and out (fig. 87.7).

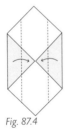

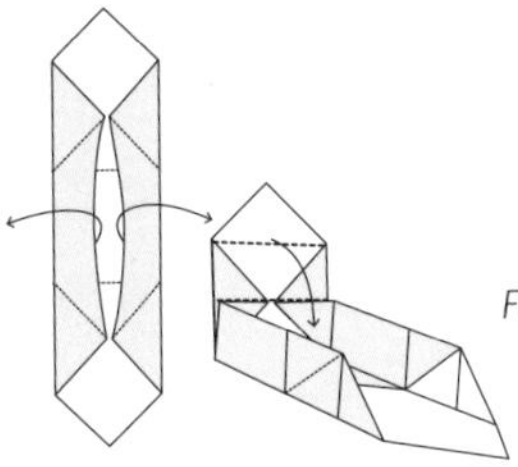

Fig. 87.7

8 Fold and tuck the bottom corner inside the box, creating the fourth side (fig. 87.8). This completes the lid of the box.

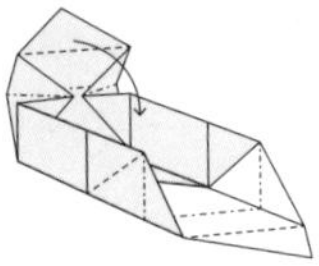

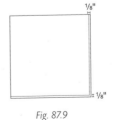

Fig. 87.8

9 To ensure that the base of the box will fit inside the lid, use scissors to trim ⅛" from two adjacent sides of the second 6" x 6" sheet (fig. 87.9). Then repeat steps 1 through 8 to complete the base of the box. Slide the lid over the base and set them aside.

⅛"

⅛"

Fig. 87.9

10 Cut two 1" x 6" sheets from the scrap paper. Accordion-fold both pieces lengthwise every ¼" (fig. 87.10).

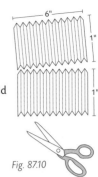

Fig. 87.10

11 Hot glue one end of one accordion-folded piece to one end of the second piece. Then hot glue the remaining ends together so the two pieces fan out to form a circle (fig. 87.11).

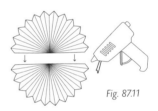

Fig. 87.11

12 Hole punch a 1" circle from the scraps of paper. Center and glue it on the fanned-out circle to complete the medallion (fig. 87.12). Then center and glue the medallion onto the lid of the box.

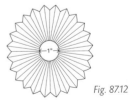

Fig. 87.12

WHAT YOU NEED

· ·

(makes 1 pinwheel)

- Glue stick

- Two 6" × 6" squares of
  paper, in contrasting
  colors or patterns

- Pencil

- Ruler

- Scissors

- Straight pin

- Hot glue gun and glue

- Drinking straw

88 | **Spinning Pinwheels**

LEVEL ✖✖✖✖✖

Pinwheels remind me of childhood summers spent playing on the beach. There is something so peaceful and mesmerizing about watching a pinwheel twirl in the breeze. While pinwheels are a great project to make with kids (just make sure *you* complete the pinning and hot gluing part), they also function as brilliant DIY summer party decor. Plant a few of them in a zinc bucket filled with sand for a table centerpiece or give them away as favors at an outdoor wedding! Oh, and a tip: I like to use paper straws for my pinwheels—so much cuter than plastic!

Back to the Fold

While traditional origami folds have no known inventors and are passed down anonymously, many modern origami artists believe that their models should be copyrighted. The very new idea that the creativity in origami should be credited to the creator represents a huge paradigm shift.

1. Spread glue stick over the wrong side of one of the sheets of paper and stick it to the wrong side of the second sheet, lining up the edges.

2. Fold the square in half diagonally and crease, then unfold. Fold along the other diagonal and crease, then unfold (fig. 88.2).

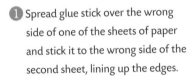

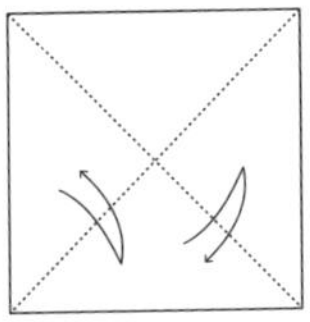

Fig. 88.2

3. Use the pencil to mark ½" from the center along each fold line (fig. 88.3).

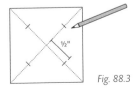

½"

Fig. 88.3

4. Use scissors to cut along the folds, starting at each corner and stopping at the marks (fig. 88.4).

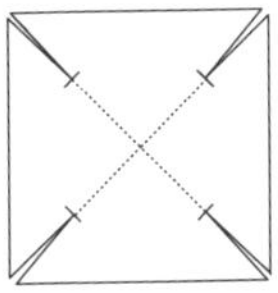

Fig. 88.4

5. Gently curl every other point into the center (fig. 88.5) and poke the pin through the tip of each point and then through the center of the pinwheel.

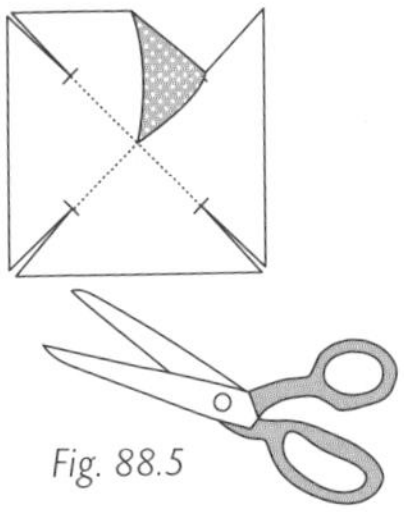

Fig. 88.5

6. Dab a tiny bit of hot glue on the tip of the pin and pierce through the straw, about 1" from the top (fig. 88.6).

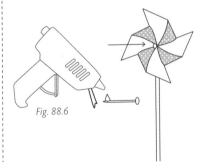

Fig. 88.6

Paper for Parties | 207

89 The Bee's Knees Piñata

LEVEL ✖ ✖ ✖ ✖ ⊗

Truth be told, I'm not a huge fan of store-bought piñatas. They often look like tacky parade floats, and they're sometimes filled with plastic toys and inedible candy. See where I'm going with this? If you make your own, you can have whatever shape piñata you want, in whatever colors you choose, and fill it up with whatever you want to rain down on you (and subsequently eat up!) after you smash it. Since piñatas are normally hung from the branch of a tree, I decided to make a piñata that mimics something that might naturally be found in a tree—a beehive!

- Newspaper
- 2 cups flour
- 1 cup water
- Mixing bowl
- Large round balloon
- Scissors
- Candy and/or toys
- Craft knife
- 4 yards twine or string
- Yellow tissue paper
- Foam brush
- Toothpick
- White glue
- Black tissue paper
- Access to a computer with a printer and paper
- Bee wings template*

1 Tear the newspaper into 1"-wide strips.

2 Mix 2 cups flour and 1 cup water together in the bowl to make a paste.

3 Inflate the balloon and tie the end.

4 One at a time, dip the newspaper strips into the paste, smooth off the excess paste, and lay them over the surface of the balloon (fig. 89.4).

5 Cover the balloon with three complete coats of strips, allowing each coat to dry completely. Snip the balloon to pop it and to allow the inside of the paper shell to dry (fig. 89.5).

Fig. 89.5

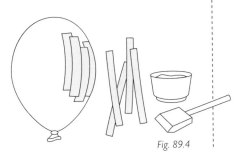

Fig. 89.4

6 Fill the piñata with candy and/or toys, cover over the opening with a layer of newspaper strips, and paste. Let dry, then add two more coats of newspaper strips, letting it dry in between coats (fig. 89.6).

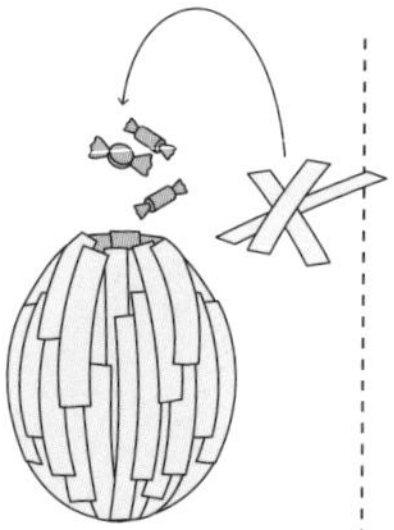

Fig. 89.6

7 Use the craft knife to poke two holes, about 2" apart, at the top of the piñata (the rounder end). Thread the twine through both holes and tie the ends in an overhand knot on the outside of the piñata. Cover the holes with two more layers of newspaper strips, paste, and let dry.

8 Cut the yellow tissue paper into ½"-wide strips. Then cut a 2" circle from the tissue paper.

9 Mix ¼ cup flour and ⅛ cup water together in a bowl to make another small amount of paste. Brush the bottom of the piñata with the paste and center the 2" circle onto it (fig. 89.9).

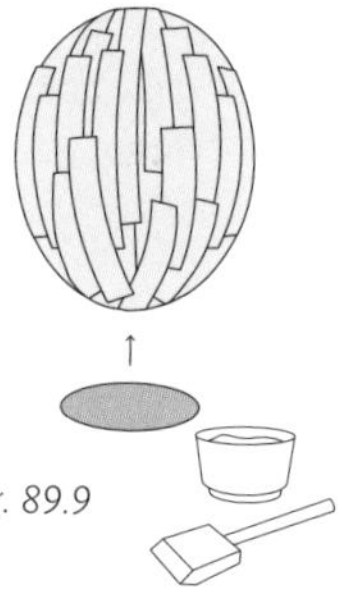

Fig. 89.9

10 Apply more paste around the circle and attach one strip of tissue paper, spiraling it tightly around the circle, to cover the newspaper.

11 Overlap the end of each strip about 1" with the beginning of a new strip, and keep adding paste and tissue paper strips until the hive is covered (fig. 89.11). At the top, carefully work around the twine. Set aside.

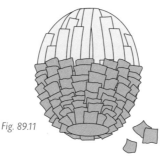

Fig. 89.11

12 Layer together five sheets of yellow tissue paper and cut a 2" × 12" strip that tapers at one end to make a long triangle (fig. 89.12).

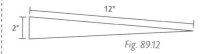

2" | 12"

Fig. 89.12

13 Keeping the layers together, start with the 2" end and roll the strips around the toothpick. Secure the ends with glue, and remove the toothpick from the center (fig. 89.13).

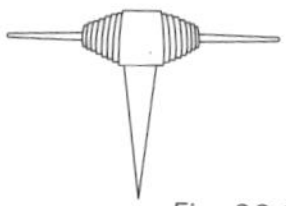

Fig. 89.13

14 Cut two ½" strips of black tissue paper and wrap them, evenly spaced, around the yellow bee body, securing the ends with glue (fig. 89.14).

Fig. 89.14

15 Repeat steps 12 through 14 to make two more bee bodies.

16 Print the bee wings template and cut it out using scissors. Trace the template on white card stock and cut the three wings out (fig. 89.16).

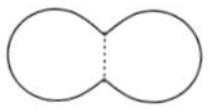

Fig. 89.16

17 Fold one pair of wings in half and brush the crease with white glue. Press it, centered, to one of the bee bodies (fig. 89.17). Repeat to assemble the remaining two sets of wings and bee bodies.

Fig. 89.17

18 Brush the bottom of the bees with white glue and stick them to the beehive (fig. 89.18). Let dry.

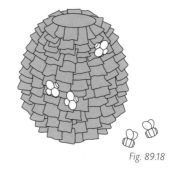

Fig. 89.18

90 | Lots of Dots Garland

LEVEL ⊗ ⊗ ⊗ ⊗ ⊗

I have a major magazine addiction. Every six months or so, I go through the giant pile, tearing out all the stuff I like and recycling the rest. But you know what's even better than recycling? Using your trash to make something useful and beautiful. These delicate strands of garland are an elegant addition to parties and holiday decor or just to spruce up your pad.

1. Trace and cut about one hundred eighty 1½"-diameter circles of varying colors from a magazine, using scissors (or cut them out using a circle cutter) (fig. 90.1).

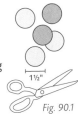

Fig. 90.1

2. Stack the circles into pairs, and use the sewing machine to sew a running or straight stitch down the center of each circle pair to join them (fig. 90.2). Clip the threads, and repeat until all the circles have been stitched.

3. Fold out the sides of each sewn circle to separate the layers, creating an X shape in the cross-section (fig. 90.3).

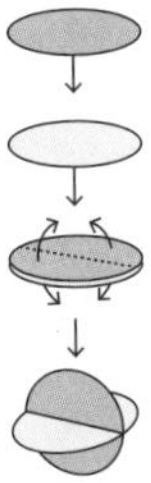

Fig. 90.2–3

4. Squeeze a few dots of hot glue down the seam line of one of the circle pieces and press it onto the twine about 3" from one end (fig. 90.4).

5. Continue gluing circle pieces to the twine, spacing them 1" apart, until the circle pieces have all been placed (fig. 90.5).

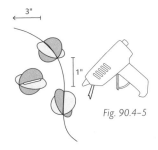

Fig. 90.4–5

WHAT YOU NEED

- Pencil
- Scissors or 1½" circle cutter
- A magazine
- Access to a sewing machine and thread (any color)
- Hot glue gun and glue
- 5 yards baker's twine or string

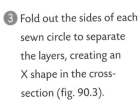

91 | Punchy Plaid Luminaria

LEVEL ●●○○○

I'm pretty much mad for plaid, and the geometric cutouts in this project remind me of a modern, abstract tartan. For your next dinner party, add these paper luminarias. They are simple to make and they twinkle magically when lit. Plus, everyone looks better by candlelight, right?

WHAT YOU NEED

- Ruler
- Glass candleholder
- Craft knife
- Self-healing cutting mat
- 1 sheet of decorative paper at least 1" wider and 2" taller than the candleholder
- Pencil
- Scissors
- Baker's twine

1 Measure the height (y) and circumference (x) of the glass candleholder. Add 2" to the height and 1" to the circumference. Use the ruler, craft knife, and cutting mat to measure and cut the paper to the revised dimensions (fig. 91.1).

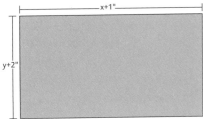

Fig. 91.1

2 Starting at one of the short ends, accordion-fold the paper every ½" to create a folded strip (fig. 91.2).

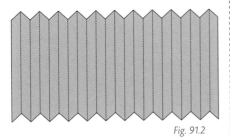

Fig. 91.2

3 Mark and snip three evenly spaced V-shaped notches along each folded side of the strip (fig. 91.3). Unfold the strip to reveal three rows of evenly spaced diamond-shaped holes in the paper.

Fig. 91.3

4 Cut three lengths of twine 4" longer than the original width of the paper. Starting at one end of the paper, weave each piece in and out of one row of holes (fig. 91.4).

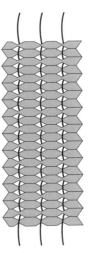

Fig. 91.4

5 Wrap the folded paper piece around the glass candleholder and tie the ends of the strings together. Arrange the folds of paper around the glass (fig. 91.5).

Fig. 91.5

92 First-Prize Paper Ribbons

LEVEL ⊗⊗⊗⊗⊗

WHAT YOU NEED

• *Scissors*

• *A few colors of crepe paper (if you can't find crepe paper, try party streamers)*

• *Decorative-edge scissors (optional)*

• *Hot glue gun and glue*

• *Scrap paper*

Prize ribbons are experiencing a major moment in the design world, and it makes sense to me: They are pretty, colorful, and they make you feel like a winner. I can think of about a million festive uses for paper prize ribbons. They make great gift toppers, party or wedding accents, or a few of them could be hung up for a nontraditional bit of wall decor. There are lots of minor variations on prize ribbons (as you can see from the photos here), so to get you started, these instructions are for the large prize ribbon on the left. Traditionally, prize ribbons are made with, well, ribbon, but it's easy to make them from crepe and scrap paper, too.

1 Cut a 2" × 25" piece of crepe paper, making sure that the grain of the paper runs the short way. Then cut a 1½" × 20" piece of crepe paper in a different color (fig. 92.1). *Optional:* Trim one long edge of each strip of paper with decorative-edge scissors.

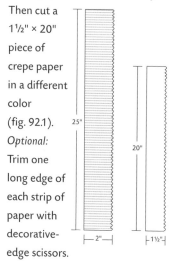

Fig. 92.1

2 Lay out the 2" × 25" piece of crepe paper lengthwise, and starting at the top short edge, fold ¼" of the paper under to the wrong side. Start making ¼" wide, slightly angled folds every ½" on the right side of the paper. With every fold, add a small dot of hot glue under the fold on the front and back of the paper. You will notice that the paper starts to curl into a rosette toward the right as you fold (fig. 92.2).

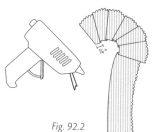

Fig. 92.2

3 When you get all the way around to make a circle, trim the paper strip, leaving a ½" tail. Fold that tail under to the wrong side, secure with hot glue, and then add one more dot of hot glue to connect the rosette together (fig. 92.3).

Fig. 92.3

4 Repeat for the smaller piece of crepe paper. Glue the smaller rosette to the larger (fig. 92.4).

5 Cut a small circle from scrap paper to cover the center of the rosette (fig. 92.5).

Fig. 92.4–5

6 Cut three pieces of crepe paper that are about 1¼" wide and as long as desired. Cut a V-shape into one end of the paper or cut them at an angle. Fan them out slightly and glue to the back of the assembled rosettes (fig. 92.6).

Fig. 92.6

7 Cut a circle from scrap paper that is large enough to cover the back of the large rosette so that you don't see any of the back of your work. Hot glue this circle to the back of the large rosette (fig. 92.7).

Fig. 92.7

WHAT YOU NEED

....

- *Foam brush*

- *White glue*

- *2 sheets of paper in different colors and/or patterns*

- *Book or other heavy, flat object (optional)*

- *Ruler*

- *Craft knife*

- *Self-healing cutting mat*

- *¼" hole punch*

- *2 small brads*

93 | Around the Globe Ornament

LEVEL ✪ ✪ ✪ ✪ ✪

These simple ornaments can be made by the dozens and hung from window frames, from a bundle of sticks in a vase, as a mobile—the point is, they are stunning when gathered together. The materials above will get you through the construction of one ornament, but they're so irresistible, you'll be doubling and tripling and quintupling your efforts in no time.

1. Brush a thin layer of glue onto the back of one sheet of paper to coat it, and press it onto the back of the second sheet, making sure to line up the edges. Let dry (fig. 93.1). *Optional:* Use a heavy object, like a book, to keep it flat while it dries.

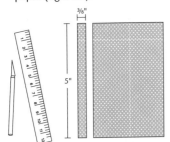

Fig. 93.1

2. Use the ruler, craft knife, and cutting mat to cut twelve ³⁄₈" × 5" strips from the new hybrid sheet of paper (fig. 93.2).

Fig. 93.2

3. Use the hole punch to make a hole about ¼" from the edge at both ends of each strip (fig. 93.3).

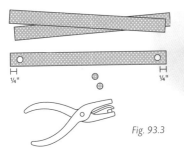

Fig. 93.3

4. Stack the twelve strips, alternating which side of the strip is visible, and line up the punched holes.

5. Push one brad through all the holes on one end and open the prongs to secure it. Repeat with the second brad on the opposite end (fig. 93.5).

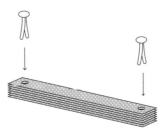

Fig. 93.5

6. Carefully separate each strip at the center, arranging them in a circle to form a globe (fig. 93.6). Hang a thread from the top.

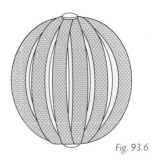

Fig. 93.6

Paper Party Props

W H A T   Y O U   N E E D

(makes 8 different costume props)

- *Access to a computer with a printer and paper*
- *Prop templates**
- *Scissors*
- *Pencil*
- *Newspaper*
- *Glue stick*
- *Card stock*
- *Ruler*
- *Hot glue gun and glue*
- *2 small binder clips (for the necktie and the bow tie)*
- *¼" circle hole punch*
- *Elastic (for the beard and eye patch)*

Photo booths: They're all the rage right now—at parties, weddings, even bridal showers! Take your photo booth extravaganza to the next level with these DIY paper props, and watch your guests—and the camera- light up with inspiration. After the excitement is over, frame your favorite photos for a charming reminder of your ultrafun bash. Since time is of the essence when you're planning any sort of shindig, these props are a cinch to put together, and they use materials that you already have lying around.

* Download at workman.com/papermade

To make a very big necktie

1. Print the prop necktie templates, cut them out with the scissors, and tape them together.

2. Trace the templates onto a piece of newspaper and cut them out. Use the glue stick to attach the back of the newspaper to a piece of card stock (you may have to piece two sheets together) and cut the shape out again. Fold the shape into a tie using the dotted guidelines on the template (fig. 94.1.2).

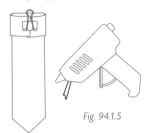

Fig. 94.1.2

3. Cut a 6" square piece of newspaper. Fold it in half, unfold it, and then fold the top and bottom edges to meet the center crease (fig. 94.1.3).

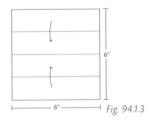

Fig. 94.1.3

4. Wrap the folded piece around the top of the necktie, hiding the "seam," and hot glue the ends in the back to create the "knot" (fig. 94.1.4).

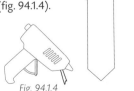

Fig. 94.1.4

5. Squeeze hot glue onto one side of a small binder clip, center, and press it into the back of the knot (fig. 94.1.5). The clip-on necktie can be easily clipped onto a shirt!

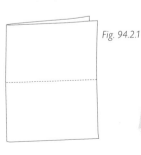

Fig. 94.1.5

To make a very big bow tie

1. Select one sheet of newspaper and fold it in half and then half again (the way a newspaper is typically folded) (fig 94.2.1).

Fig. 94.2.1

2. Starting at one of the long edges, make ½" accordion-style folds in the folded sheet (fig. 94.2.2).

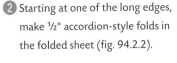
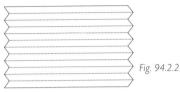

Fig. 94.2.2

3. From a second sheet of newspaper, cut a 2" x 8" strip, and fold it in half lengthwise.

4. Wrap it around the center of the accordion-folded paper. Hot glue the ends of the strips in the back to create the "knot" (fig. 94.2.4).

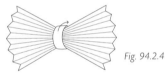

Fig. 94.2.4

5. Squeeze hot glue onto one side of a small binder clip and center and press it into the back of the knot. Gently pull apart the folds to fluff up the bow tie and clip it on!

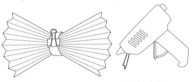

Fig. 94.2.5

To make a beard

1. Print the beard template and cut it out with the scissors.

2. Trace the template onto a piece of newspaper and roughly cut it out. Coat the back of the newspaper beard with glue stick and press it onto the card stock. Cut it out (fig. 94.3.2).

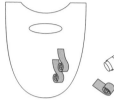

Fig. 94.3.2

3. Cut dozens of ½" × 2" strips of newspaper. One at a time, wrap each strip around the pencil to curl it (fig. 94.3.3).

Fig. 94.3.3

4. Spread glue stick on one end of a curled strip and attach it to the front of the beard panel (fig. 94.3.4). Repeat to cover the entire panel with curls.

Fig. 94.3.4

5. Punch a hole on either side of the top of the beard, about ½" from the edge, as marked on the template.

6. Cut a piece of elastic and tie each end through one of the holes, leaving enough length to fit comfortably around the back of one's head (fig. 94.3.6).

Fig. 94.3.6

To make a pirate hat

1. Print the pirate hat template and skull and crossbones template and cut them out with the scissors.

2. Trace the hat template on a piece of newspaper, then flip it over and trace it again to make the front side of the hat. Repeat to make the back side (fig. 94.4.2).

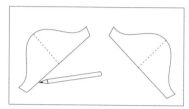

Fig. 94.4.2

3. Cut the hat pieces out roughly, and use glue stick to attach them to the card stock. Cut out the stiffened pieces.

4. Trace the skull and crossbones templates onto card stock and cut them out. Spread glue stick across the back of the skull and crossbones, center, and stick on the front of one of the hat pieces (fig. 94.4.4).

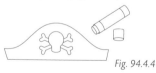

Fig. 94.4.4

5. Select a full sheet of newspaper and fold it in half diagonally (fig. 94.4.5). Crease it.

Fig. 94.4.5

6 Starting at the crease, do a rolling fold every 2" until you reach the point(s). Secure the point(s) in place with glue stick (fig. 94.4.6).

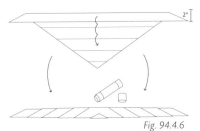

Fig. 94.4.6

7 Wrap the folded strip to create a band, overlap, and hot glue the ends together (fig. 94.4.7).

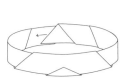

Fig. 94.4.7

8 Squeeze a line of hot glue across the front of the band and attach the pirate hat front. Repeat on the back of the band with the pirate hat back (fig. 94.4.8).

Fig. 94.4.8

To make a flapper headband

1 Select a full sheet of newspaper and follow steps 5 through 7 of the pirate hat instructions to make a band (fig. 94.4.5–7).

2 Print the feather template and cut it out with the scissors.

3 Spread glue stick across a piece of newspaper and attach to a piece of card stock. Trace the three feather templates onto the card stock side and cut them out. Cut fringe along the edges of each, using the markings on the template as a guide (fig. 94.5.3).

4 Mark and cut a 2" circle from the newspaper and cut fringe around the edge (fig. 94.5.4).

Fig. 94.5.3–4

5 Squeeze hot glue onto the ends of the feathers and stick them to the front of the band. Glue the circle over the bottoms of the feathers (fig. 94.5.5).

Fig. 94.5.5

flapper headband

These are fun to make for any party!

To make a sailor's hat

1. Select a full sheet of newspaper and fold it in half along the natural fold of the paper (fig. 94.6.1).

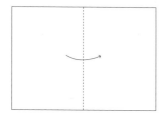

Fig. 94.6.1

2. Rotate the paper so the fold is at the top. Fold the top left and right points down to meet in the center (fig. 94.6.2).

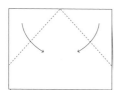

Fig. 94.6.2

3. Fold the bottom flap up, partially covering the folded flaps from step 2 (fig. 94.6.3).

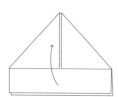

Fig. 94.6.3

4. Flip the hat over and fold the bottom flap up (fig. 94.6.4).

Fig. 94.6.4

To make a party hat

1. Print the party hat template and cut it out with the scissors.

2. The template represents one third of the party hat, so trace the template three times (fig. 94.7.2). Roughly cut out the shape.

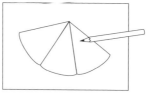

Fig. 94.7.2

3. Spread glue stick over the back of the shape and press it onto a piece of card stock. Cut it out.

4. Curve the shape into a cone. Squeeze a line of hot glue along one of the straight edges and overlap the edges to secure them (fig. 94.7.4).

Fig. 94.7.4

5. Snip off ½" from the top of the cone (fig. 94.7.5).

Fig. 94.7.5

6. Cut three 2"-wide strips the length of a newspaper. Stack them and cut fringe into one long edge, through all three layers, from one end of the strip to the other (fig. 94.7.6).

Fig. 94.7.6

sailor's hat

party hat

To make an eye patch

① Print the eye patch template and cut it out with the scissors.

② Trace the template three times onto a sheet of newspaper and use the scissors to cut them out. Spread glue stick on each piece and stack them (fig. 94.8.2).

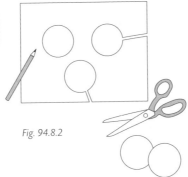

Fig. 94.8.2

❖

Now *Hat's* Entertainment!

There was once a time when a well-heeled lady wouldn't leave the house without a hat. In the early 1900s every woman wanted a big and bold hat. The only problem: These hats came at a price. A few resourceful paper companies saw a niche market and started publishing instructions for crepe paper hats. In a few steps, women could make themselves a closet full of hats in every trend and shape for a fraction of the price of one by a hatmaker.

⑦ Roll up the stacked strip and secure the end with a dab of glue stick (fig. 94.7.7).

Fig. 94.7.7

⑧ Spread glue over the ends of the rolled paper and insert the roll into the top of the cone, fringe side up (fig. 94.7.8). Fluff out the rolled paper to make the pom-pom.

Fig. 94.7.8

③ Cut a 1" slit from the edge of the eye patch into the center (fig. 94.8.3).

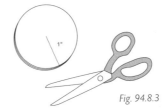

Fig. 94.8.3

④ Overlap the edges of the slit slightly and glue to shape the eye patch (fig. 94.8.4)

Fig. 94.8.4

⑤ Use the hole punch to make holes on either side of the eye patch

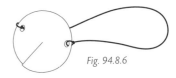

Fig. 94.8.5

(fig. 94.8.5). Cut a piece of elastic long enough to fit securely around an average-size head (about 22").

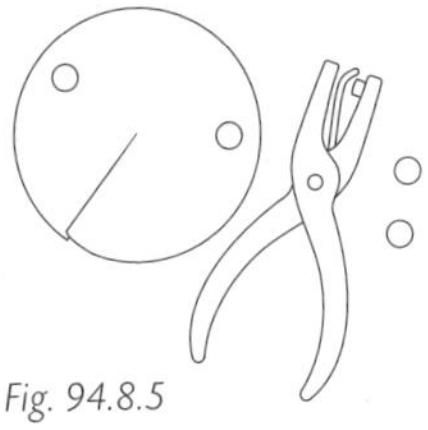

⑥ Thread one end of the elastic through each of the two holes on the eye patch and tie a knot at each end (fig. 94.8.6).

Fig. 94.8.6

95 | Pin the Hat on Aunt Hattie Game

LEVEL ⊗ ⊗ ⊗ ⊗ ⊗

So much more fun than Pin the Tail on the Donkey! While the more traditional game is ubiquitous at kids' parties, I can't see why adults shouldn't enjoy a few rounds of what I like to call Pin the Hat on Aunt Hattie (or Glasses on Aunt Gladys, Bow Tie on Uncle Bob—the variations are endless!), especially after a couple of cocktails.

WHAT YOU NEED

- 1 *hi-res photo of the person you would like to pin something on*
- *Access to a large printer or a copy shop*
- *Hat templates**
- *Tracing paper*
- *Pencil*
- *Scissors*
- *Decorative-edge scissors*
- *Scraps of colored card stock*
- *Glue stick*
- *Thumbtacks*
- *Double-stick tape (optional)*

1 Select a photo of the person who's getting pinned and then have the photo enlarged to poster size (fig. 95.1).

Fig. 95.1

2 Print the hat templates and cut them out. *Optional:* Choose an alternate accessory for the subject in the poster—a pair of glasses, a beehive hairdo, a tie, a beard, and so on, and draw and cut it out.

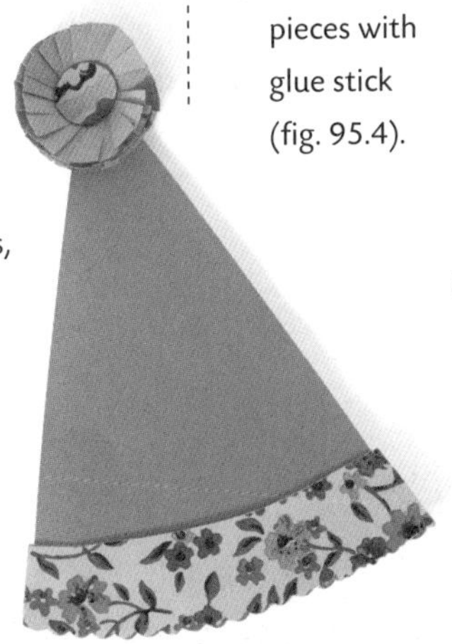

3 Trace the template pieces onto colored card stock and cut them out (fig. 95.3).

Fig. 95.3

4 Assemble the pieces with glue stick (fig. 95.4).

Fig. 95.4

5 To play the game, pin the poster to the wall, blindfold your guests, spin them around, and challenge them to pin or tape (place a piece of double-stick tape on the back of the paper accessory if you're playing with small children) the hat (hairdo, tie, glasses, or beard) to the poster (fig. 95.5).

Fig. 95.5

* Download at workman.com/papermade

96

Jacob's Ladder Chain

LEVEL ✪ ✪ ✪ ✪ ✪

Remember those standard-issue, stapled construction paper chains that you made in elementary school? Why not refresh the old idea with new materials? A Jacob's ladder chain is a fantastic way to repurpose old magazines, office papers, newspapers, and any other paper scraps into festive decorations. You can hang them in windows, from the edges of lampshades, or coil them in a dish—bright accents that can be placed anywhere!

WHAT YOU NEED

- Ruler
- Craft knife
- Self-healing cutting mat
- Scraps of paper (magazine, newspaper, or gift paper)
- Small brush
- White glue
- Scissors

❶ Use the ruler, craft knife, and cutting mat to cut thirty ½"-wide strips of paper.

❷ Brush glue onto the end of one paper strip. Press the end of a second paper strip into the glue at a right angle (fig. 96.2).

Fig. 96.2

❸ Fold the first strip over the second strip, keeping the strips at a right angle, and crease. Continue folding the strips over each other at right angles (fig. 96.3).

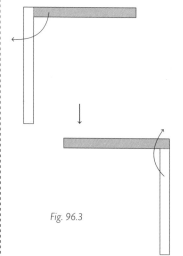

Fig. 96.3

❹ To extend a strip, snip the end of one strip so that it falls halfway across the other strip. Brush the end with glue, and press a new strip so that it extends in the same direction.

❺ Continue folding the chain and adding strips until the supply of paper strips is exhausted. Then trim the ends and glue them together, overlapping, to complete the chain (fig. 96.5).

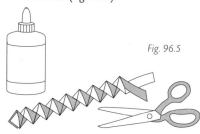

Fig. 96.5

97

Pajaki Chandelier

LEVEL ⊗ ⊗ ⊗ ⊗ ⊗

WHAT YOU NEED

- Ruler
- Scissors
- Tissue paper in a variety of colors
- 9" embroidery hoop
- Small paintbrush
- White glue
- Pencil
- Scraps of paper in a variety of colors or patterns
- Decorative-edge scissors
- Round chopstick
- Thread
- Sewing needle
- C-clamp or large binder clip
- Hot glue gun and glue

The small town of Łowicz, Poland, just outside Warsaw, is known for its colorful folk art. *Pajaki* chandeliers, which literally translates to "spiders of straw" (but which look much better than that!), are their most famous craft—a cheap, colorful, and oh-so-DIY way for Polish women to decorate their homes. DIYers around the world are catching on, and it's not hard to see why: The chandeliers are fun to make and the materials are a cinch to find. Admittedly, they are a bit time-consuming, but they are the perfect project to brighten an otherwise dreary winter day.

1️⃣ Cut fifteen 1"-wide strips of tissue paper in one color.

2️⃣ Separate the outside from the inside of the embroidery hoop. (This project requires only the inside of the hoop.)

3️⃣ Using the small paintbrush, dab white glue on the inside of the hoop and begin to wrap the tissue paper strips around the hoop (fig. 97.3).

Fig. 97.3

4️⃣ When you reach the end of a tissue paper strip, secure the end with glue on the inside of the hoop and overlap another strip, keeping the seam hidden. Continue wrapping until the whole hoop is covered. Set it aside.

5️⃣ Trace seventy-five 1" circles and one 3" circle on different colored paper. Cut them out with decorative-edge scissors (fig. 97.5).

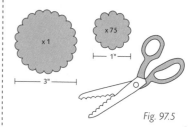

Fig. 97.5

6 Mark six evenly spaced dots ½" from the edge of the 3" circle. Set the circles aside (fig. 97.6).

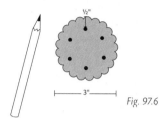

Fig. 97.6

7 Cut eighty-two 1" square pieces of paper. Roll each square around a chopstick to make a small tube, and secure the edges with glue to create short paper straws (fig. 97.7). Set them aside. *Note: Traditionally, these round spacers on the chandelier are made with cut straw. Paper makes a colorful substitute.*

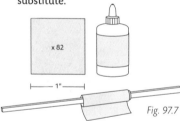

Fig. 97.7

8 Cut forty-two 3" × 6" strips of tissue paper in various colors.

9 Stack six strips together and fold them accordion-style from one short end with ½" folds (fig. 97.9).

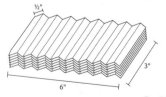

Fig. 97.9

10 Cut small V-shape notches into the strip at the center of each folded edge (fig. 97.10).

Fig. 97.10

11 Wrap a small length of thread around the folded strip at the notches. Fan out the fold and gently separate each layer to make a flower (fig. 97.11).

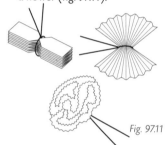

Fig. 97.11

12 Repeat steps 8 through 11 six times to complete seven flowers.

13 Cut eighteen 2" × 3" squares of tissue paper and repeat steps 9 through 11 to make three smaller flowers.

14 Thread the needle. Leaving 12" of thread at each end for tying, string six strands of seven 1" circles and eight paper straws. Start with a straw and alternate the pieces (fig. 97.14).

Fig. 97.14   × 6

15 String three strands of four 1" paper circles and four paper straws. Start with a straw and alternate the pieces (fig. 97.15).

16 String three strands of six 1" circles and seven paper straws. Start with two straws and alternate the pieces (fig. 97.16).

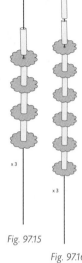

× 3

× 3

Fig. 97.15

Fig. 97.16

17 Tie the six strands of seven 1" circles and eight paper straws from step 14, spacing them evenly around the embroidery hoop (fig. 97.17).

Fig. 97.17

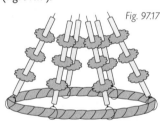

18 One at a time, thread the top of each strand with the needle and insert it through one of the marked dots in the 3" paper circle from step 6 (fig. 97.18).

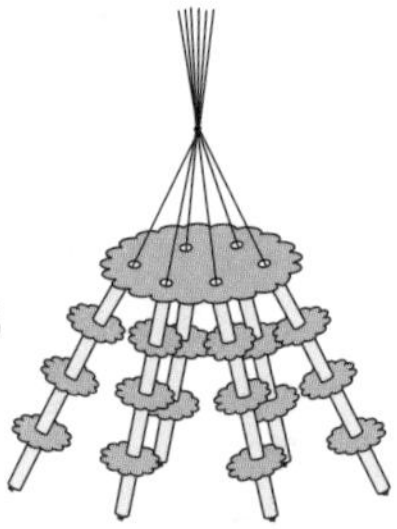

Fig. 97.18

19 Grasp the ends of the six threads in your hand, make sure all the strands are hanging evenly, and overhand knot. Then thread all six strands through a paper straw to hide the knot (fig. 97.19).

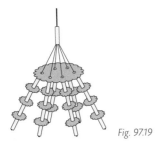

Fig. 97.19

20 Use the C-clamp to hang the chandelier on a ledge or shelf to continue assembly.

21 Alternating where the six strands are tied to the embroidery hoop, tie on the three strands of four 1" paper circles and four paper straws from step 15 (fig. 97.21).

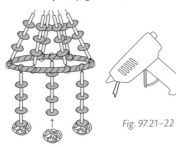

Fig. 97.21–22

22 Squeeze a dot of hot glue to attach the three smaller paper flowers to the bottom circle at the end of each of those three strands (fig. 97.22).

23 Use hot glue to attach six large tissue paper flowers around the outside of the embroidery hoop, lining them up with the tied strands (fig. 97.23).

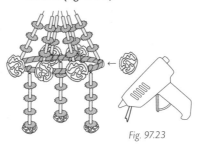

Fig. 97.23

24 In between the large tissue paper flowers along the embroidery hoop, tie the three strands of six circles and seven straws from step 16 (fig. 97.24).

25 Gather together the ends of the three hanging strands, knot them, and hot glue the last large flower to the knot, connecting the strands and concealing the knot (fig. 97.25).

Fig. 97.24–25

26 One at a time, hot glue three 1" paper circles along the outside of the embroidery hoop to conceal the three knots made in step 24 (fig. 97.26).

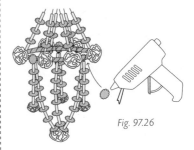

Fig. 97.26

27 Unclamp the chandelier and find a more permanent display location!

98 | Leaf Peeper Wreath

LEVEL ✪ ✪ ✪ ○ ○

I grew up in New England, and the first few weeks of fall were always my favorite time of the year. The turning leaves are especially vibrant in the Northeast. It's all highlighted by a crispness in the air, that heady smell of falling leaves and ripe apples, scarves and boots and tweed jackets—I love it all! This wreath is a yearlong reminder of the colors of fall, and might conjure some of those other elements of autumn, too.

WHAT YOU NEED

- Access to a computer with a printer and paper
- Leaf templates*
- Craft knife
- Self-healing cutting mat
- Pencil
- Scraps of paper (at least 3" to 4") in a variety of colors and patterns
- ½" circle hole punch
- 8" embroidery hoop or metal hoop
- Hot glue gun and glue

❶ Print the leaf templates and cut them out using the craft knife and cutting mat. Make sure to cut out the vein details, too.

❷ Trace the templates a total of forty times onto different papers. Trace the vein details onto about ten leaves. Cut out the leaves with a craft knife, and save the vein details removed from the leaf to use as branches (fig. 98.2).

Fig. 98.2

❸ Use the hole punch to make about eighteen berries from one of the colored papers (fig. 98.3).

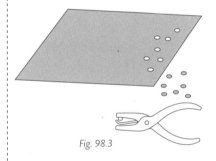

Fig. 98.3

❹ Lay the embroidery hoop flat and arrange the leaves, overlapping, around it. Hot glue the leaves in place and add branches as desired (fig. 98.4).

❺ Arrange the berries in groups of three and hot glue them around the wreath, over the leaves and branches (fig. 98.5).

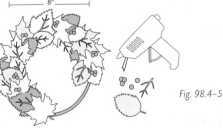

Fig. 98.4–5

* Download at workman.com/papermade

(makes 1 riser)

- 2 paperbuck books that are equal in height
- Craft knife
- Hot glue gun and glue
- Pencil
- Corrugated cardboard from one small box
- Self-healing cutting mat
- Decoupage medium
- Foam brush
- Scissors
- Access to a computer with a printer and paper
- Scallop template*

① Use the craft knife to carefully separate the covers from both paperback books (fig. 99.1). (Save the covers for another project!) Then cut seven pages from one of the books and set them aside. (These sheets will cover the top of the riser and become the scallop detail.)

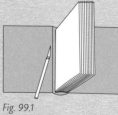

Fig. 99.1

* Download at workman.com/papermade

99 Paperback Riser

LEVEL ✪ ✪ ✪ ✪ ○

A cake stand functions to elevate a cake (both literally and aesthetically), but a cake stand made of paperback books really *rises* to the occasion! While one stand is dandy, try several cake stands at varying heights (use different size books) for an event showstopper.

❷ Lay one book flat. Select about five pages and roll the outer edge of the page packet into the spine of the book without creasing (fig. 99.2).

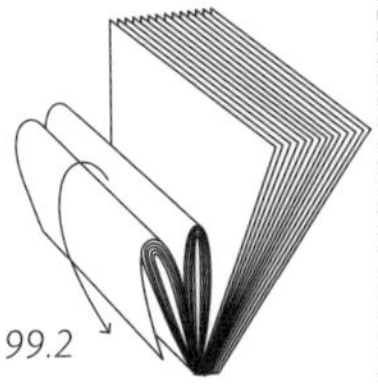

Fig. 99.2

❸ Repeat step 2 until you reach the back of the book and all the page packets have been looped.

❹ Repeat steps 2 and 3 with the second book. Squeeze hot glue generously along the binding of one of the looped books and press it into the other binding (fig. 99.4). Hot glue the end pages of one book to the other to reinforce.

Fig. 99.4

❺ Trace a 9"- or 10"-diameter circle onto the cardboard. Use the craft knife and cutting mat to carefully cut out the circle.

❻ Select six of the reserved book pages from step 1 and tear them into ½"-wide strips.

❼ Use decoupage medium and a foam brush to apply the strips across one side of the cardboard circle. Wrap the ends of the strips around the edges of the circle, to conceal the cardboard. Let dry (fig. 99.7).

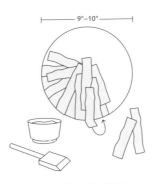

9"–10"

Fig. 99.7

❽ With the remaining paper strips, cover the other side of the circle too, trimming off any excess paper. Let dry.

❾ Brush another coat of decoupage medium over the front and back of the circle. Let dry.

❿ Print the scallop template and cut it out. Trace the template four to five times onto the remaining book page, moving the template as you trace to make continuous strips the length of the page (fig. 99.10).

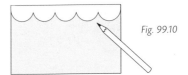

Fig. 99.10

⓫ Cut out the scalloped trim. Check that you have between 29" and 32" combined to wrap around the edge of the circle. Trace and cut more if necessary.

⓬ Squeeze hot glue across the top of the book assembly and press the cardboard circle, centered, on top (fig. 99.12).

⓭ Hot glue the straight edge of the scallop trim around the edge of the circle (fig. 99.13).

Fig. 99.12–13

(makes 1 six-piece set)

- *Access to a computer with a printer and paper*
- *Large and small circle templates**
- *Scissors*
- *Scraps of solid and patterned paper (card stock or the inside of security envelopes from the junk mail pile work well)*
- *Pencil*
- *Glue stick*
- *¼" circle hole punch*
- *Baker's twine or string*

100 | Cute as a Button Napkin Rings

LEVEL ⊗ ⊗ ⊗ ⊗ ⊗

Napkin rings can be cumbersome for day-to-day use, but they are invaluable when it comes to big parties. Party rental linens are available in a pretty limited spectrum of colors and patterns, and they usually need more than a little styling help! These totally cute (as a button) napkin rings are perfect for both kids and adults alike, and they do a lot to dress up those plain Jane napkins. If you're not planning on using napkin rings for your party, tie the buttons as charms around the stems of the wine glasses.

1. Print the large and small circle templates and cut them out using scissors. Select the papers you want to use for the napkin rings and trace one large and one small circle per napkin ring. *Note:* Trace twelve total circles for a set of six napkin rings.

2. Cut out the circles. Spread glue stick evenly on the back of each of the small circles and press them, centered, onto the large circles (fig. 100.2).

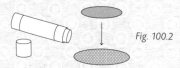

Fig. 100.2

3. Determine whether the buttons will have two or four holes, and mark the holes on the inner circle with the pencil. Then use the hole punch to punch them out (fig. 100.3).

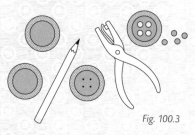

Fig. 100.3

* Download at workman.com/papermade

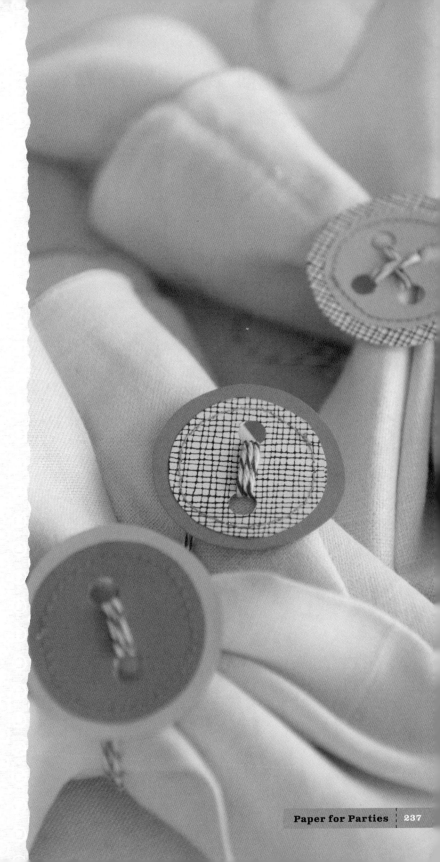

4 To attach the button to a rolled napkin, rest the button on the napkin and thread a piece of twine up through one of the holes (fig. 100.4a). Thread it back down through the hole diagonal to the first, then wrap it around the back of the napkin and up through an adjacent hole. Cross the twine over the first line of twine and down through the remaining hole. Tie the ends at the back of the napkin (fig. 100.4b). For a button with two holes, simply thread the twine up through one hole, down through the second, and tie the ends at the back of the napkin (fig. 100.4c).

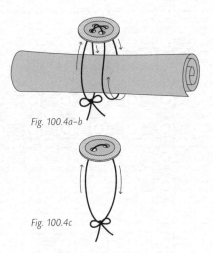

Fig. 100.4a–b

Fig. 100.4c

101 | Spin Me Right 'Round Top

LEVEL ⊗⊗⊗⊗⊗

WHAT YOU NEED
....
- *3 squares of paper (6")*

A spinning top is a fun introduction to modular origami, a paper-folding technique that uses multiple sheets of paper to create one larger complex structure. As in lots of origami, the creator of this model is unknown, but whoever the person was, I am thankful to be able to share this fun project with you. It's definitely more time-consuming than most origami, but when you're done you'll have a toy that you made yourself out of just a few sheets of paper!

Part A

1. Lay one of the paper squares flat wrong side up. Valley fold it in half, unfold, and then fold it in half again in the opposite direction (fig. 101.1). Then unfold. Repeat, folding along the diagonals.

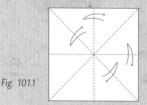

Fig. 101.1

2. Valley fold one edge in to meet the center fold, and crease (fig. 101.2). Repeat for the opposite edge.

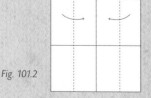

Fig. 101.2

3. Orient the folded paper vertically. Valley fold the top left corner across diagonally so that the top left half meets the center line (fig. 101.3). Crease and unfold. Repeat for the top right, bottom left, and bottom right corners.

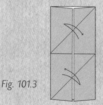

Fig. 101.3

4. Valley fold the top edge of the paper down to the center. Crease and unfold. Repeat for the bottom edge (fig. 101.4).

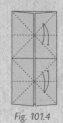

Fig. 101.4

5. Pull down the top edge to the center again and, using the folds you just made, pull out the sides to the left and right to make a trapezoidal shape. Repeat for the bottom edge (fig. 101.5).

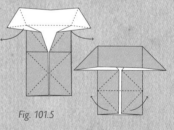

Fig. 101.5

6. Take the right point of the upper trapezoid and fold it up to form a flap. Fold the left point of the lower trapezoid down to form another flap (fig. 101.6). The paper will now resemble a windmill.

Fig. 101.6

7. Fold each flap of the windmill back onto itself to create four small squares (fig. 101.7).

Fig. 101.7

8. Bring the center point of each small square outward and cajole it into a long diamond shape (fig. 101.8).

Fig. 101.8

9. Take the point of the small triangular flaps between the long diamond shapes and fold them out as far as they'll go (fig. 101.9).

Fig. 101.9

10. Fold the tip of each diamond toward the center of the paper, so it resembles a long kite (fig. 101.10).

Fig. 101.10

Part B

11 Lay a second paper square flat, wrong side up. Fold it in half, unfold, and then fold it in half again in the opposite direction (fig. 101.11). Then unfold.

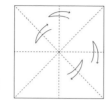

Fig. 101.11

12 Fold each corner into the center of the square to make a smaller square (fig. 101.12).

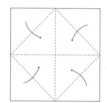

Fig. 101.12

13 Repeat step 12 to make a smaller square (fig. 101.13).

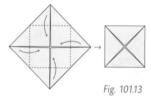

Fig. 101.13

14 Flip the paper over so all the folds are facing down and repeat step 12 again (fig. 101.14).

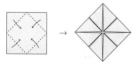

Fig. 101.14

15 Turn the square back over, flap side up. Fold out each of the flaps from the center to meet the outside point of each corner (fig. 101.15).

Fig. 101.15

Part C

16 Lay the third paper square flat, wrong side up. Fold it in half, unfold, and then fold it in half again in the opposite direction (fig. 101.16). Then unfold.

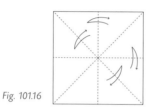

Fig. 101.16

17 Repeat step 12 three times (fig. 101.17).

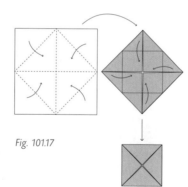

Fig. 101.17

18 Fold the small square in half, crease, and unfold. Repeat on the other half (fig. 101.18).

Fig. 101.18

19 Turn the paper over so the flaps are facing down. Push in each crease to form a four-pointed star (fig. 101.19).

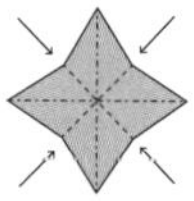

Fig. 101.19

20 To complete the top, take Part B and tuck the corners of the square into the flaps of Part A (fig. 101.20a). Then take Part C and slide the tips of the star under the flaps in Part B (fig. 101.20b). Use Part C to spin the top (fig. 101.20c)!

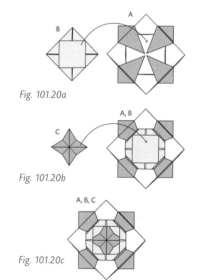

Fig. 101.20a

Fig. 101.20b

Fig. 101.20c

INDEX

· · · · · · · · · · · ·

Paper Made!

3 1901 05364 5042